Inspired

Twenty amazing real life stories that will touch your heart, rekindle your faith and even change your life

Inspired

Twenty amazing real life stories that
will touch your heart, rekindle your
faith and even change your life

alive Publishing

First published in 2018 by Alive Publishing Ltd
Graphic House, 124 City Road, Stoke on Trent, ST4 2PH
Tel: +44 (0) 1782 745600 • Fax: +44 (0) 1782 745500
email: booksales@alivepublishing.co.uk
www.alivepublishing.co.uk

© 2018 Alive Publishing. British Library Catalogue-in-
Publication Data.
A catalogue record for this book is available from the
British Library.

ISBN: 978-1-906278-33-5

Contents

Contents

Contents

Contents

Introduction

'How many celebrities have you met?' That's the question I'm often asked, when I tell people I'm a journalist. And the truth is that I have met celebrities, many of them, over three decades in the interviewing business. Some of them – most of them, perhaps – are talented people with interesting and thought-provoking observations to share.

But when it comes to the interviewees who have had most impact on my life, and whose stories I have been most privileged to share, there's no doubt about it: they're not celebrities, they're the people in this book. Ordinary people – ordinary only in the sense that they're not famous, or seeking fame, or looking for anything in life that marked them out in a public role – who found themselves up against an extraordinary situation, and had to make decisions they never expected to have to make, decisions that would not only set their lives on a whole new path, but change the lives of many others.

Often - tragically, searingly, horribly - the event that changed the lives in this book was a loss. Often, it was a loss in almost unimaginable circumstances. The father-to-be whose wife, just days away from delivering their first child, went to the shops to pick up a few groceries and was killed in a car crash (their child was born afterwards, and mercifully survived). The mother whose 16-year-old son went to the baker's shop to buy some food, and was killed by an assailant. Another mother, whose son walked into a school with a gun and shot eight little girls, killing five of them, before turning the gun on himself. The single mother whose only child died when she took a dose of ecstasy she thought was safe, but which turned out to be deadly. The priest who, having campaigned against apartheid in South Africa, thought the battle was over; until one day he opened a packet of religious magazines, and had both his hands blown off. A bomb, intended to kill him, had been hidden inside its pages.

In all these lives, everything turned on a moment: a moment that could so easily have been averted, or not have happened. Katherine Luzzi's car could have been driving along that road five minutes later and not crashed; Jimmy Mizen could have decided he didn't want a sausage roll that day. Charles Roberts could have been stopped on his journey to the school; Martha Fernback could have taken ecstasy that wasn't deadly because it was so high-grade. Fr Michael Lapsley could have decided not to bother opening the post that had piled up after he'd been away from home for several weeks.

But each of these events did happen; and in a split second, the landscape of life had changed utterly and irrevocably. The shock was indescribable; every single plan and ambition and expectation and hope these people had was changed; their entire investment in the future had been wiped out, totally changed. They had to learn to accept an unthinkable change to their life's circumstances, and to realise that things would never, ever be the same again; and then, and crucially, they had to decide how they were going to live on. And each of them decided that, though none of them wanted the changed lives they now had to live, they would

– in a way – embrace those lives, and determine to lead them as fully as possible; but more than that, in a way that allowed others to benefit from their tragedy.

That is what makes these people inspiring. Some people call them brave, but they don't think of themselves as brave, and in all honesty some of them talked to me about how terrified they felt, at various moments along the journey. And what is bravery, really, except moving forward in as positive a way as possible even when you are feeling very, very scared? Calling people 'brave' often serves to suggest that they're in some way different, that they're endowed with an extra-special ability to keep on going; but the truth is that they were ordinary people, who felt extremely frightened, but who found the strength inside themselves to not only keep on going, but to use the circumstances that had blighted their lives to help heal themselves and others.

None of us knows what we would do if we found ourselves in this sort of situation; and most of us will never suffer the headline-making events these people have suffered. But in every life there are tragedies and shocks; in every life there are traumatic and shattering moments. We must all learn to live with seismic change at some point or another: perhaps through bereavement, perhaps through a broken love affair, perhaps through being abandoned by someone we loved and thought we could trust. Because we will all experience loss; it's one of the givens of a lifetime, like being born and dying. If we live, we are born; if we live, we die. If we live, we will lose; and we will have to make choices about how to go on living with that loss in our heart. And the stories of people like Joe Luzzi and Margaret Mizen, Anne-Marie Cockburn and Michael Lapsley, can help us transform our own lives, enabling us to keep on going in the belief that we can find positivity and strength, for ourselves and for others, while not negating or ignoring the magnitude of loss in our hearts.

These stories are perhaps the most dramatic in this book: but there are many others that are equally inspiring. They're the stories of people whose lives took an unexpected turn that didn't involve a death, but did involve a total change of circumstances: circumstances that could crush many people, and that might have crushed them. I'm thinking now of people like Sunny Jacobs and Peter Pringle, both condemned to death for crimes they didn't commit; Christina Noble, wrenched from her family as a child of ten, and later told they were dead; Rachel Kelly, who found herself as a young mother hospitalised with paralysing depression and Guy Stagg, who found himself in a similar situation while at university. These people found themselves on the receiving end of events that were totally overwhelming, and must at times have seemed insurmountable; and yet, as you will read, they found a way through.

For others in this book, the circumstances that were pivotal to their lives happened early. Jessica Cox was born with no arms; Pierluigi Molla's mother went away to have a baby, when he was a young child, and died soon afterwards. From their earliest times they had to learn to live with being different: and for both, it was in acknowledging what they had to deal with that they found peace and purpose. Jessica, astonishingly, went on to become a pilot; Pierluigi saw his mother canonised in St Peter's Square in Rome.

Sometimes, for the people whose stories are told in this book, it was a chance remark that led them to change not only their own lives, but those of many others. Magnus MacFarlane-Barrow was trying to find something uplifting in a conversation with a boy whose mother had died of HIV/Aids in Malawi; Helen Prejean was hearing that there were prisoners on death row who needed people to befriend them; Jean Vanier noticed that people were being needlessly institutionalised because of mental health problems. The difficulties these people became aware of were not their own difficulties; they were problems in other people's lives that they were open to hearing about. Instead of shying away from them, they engaged with them, and allowed themselves to be pulled in. So too did Rita Lee, who set up an extraordinary food bank and soup kitchen for people in Manchester; and Angel Garcia, who opened his church in Madrid round-the-clock for homeless people in need of shelter. And Ancy Mathew, a nun in London, realised the extent of the suffering of trafficked people in her city, and that there was a role caring for them that was being overlooked.

These are all people who could have walked by on the other side, as all of us can in our lives; but they chose to cross the street, to stop, to listen and to understand the plight of others who were in need. And then they decided not to cross the street again, but to remain on the same side of it as these people, to walk with them and to be agents of real change in so many lives.

And then there are the activists: people like Teresa Forcades, a Spanish nun who works to end misogyny and injustice in her church and in her wider community; and Rose Hudson-Wilkin, who is a role model for young black women in Britain today, and who understands the power of the role model because of events in her own life and Tim Shriver, who works to change society's attitude to people with learning difficulties. Activists are people who could have chosen quieter, easier paths in life: but when they realised the need to stand up and be counted, to fly the banner for the cause they believed in, they embraced it wholeheartedly – and the world is changing for the better because of them.

Each one of these individuals has trusted me to listen to their story and to tell it, and I am immensely grateful to them. I believe that my own life has been enormously enriched by talking to them and hearing about their experiences and their choices; and I very much hope that reading what they have to share will be helpful to you as well. Perhaps you will fold their example into your heart and remember it in a moment of loss or tribulation; because that is the role inspiring stories can have in our lives. Perhaps you will take up a new cause or work for something you believe in, as so many of those in this book have done. Perhaps you will see something that you have always thought of as a difficulty or a stumbling block in your life, in a new way. In any event, I hope you find these stories, as I have done, inspiring; and I hope you allow them to touch your heart, as they deserve to do.

Joanna Moorhead
October 2018

1

The pilot who lost her arms

Jessica Cox decided at an early age that she could do anything she set her mind to. Today she flies planes – and she tours the world lecturing on the power of positive thinking, and having the faith to achieve.

The first passenger Jessica Cox took up into the skies after she got her pilot's licence was someone very special: her father Bill. He is, says Jessica, 'a bit of a control freak', so putting his life into his daughter's hands wasn't easy for him. But only figuratively speaking: because Jessica has no hands, and no arms. She was the first woman to fly a plane with her feet: and it was Bill's belief in her, from the day of her birth, that helped make her extraordinary achievement possible.

Meeting Jessica for the first time you're immediately aware of the way she's different, because she can't shake hands. Where her shoulders are she has simply shoulders; no arms. It's a shock to see, but within minutes of being with her you're at your ease.

> She looked at my dad and she said, you know what? You must be pretty special parents for God to bless you with a child like this one

Jessica is friendly, engaging, lively and fun; and everything about her conveys the message she wants you to get, which is that having no arms is no big deal for her, so it shouldn't be for you either.

Jessica's parents had no idea she had no arms until she was born, by Caesarean section, 32 years ago. 'It was the days before ultrasound scans were very advanced so they had no reason to suspect anything was wrong. And when I came out everyone was completely shocked. When the doctor told my mum I had no arms she just fell apart – she was sobbing and shaking. But my dad didn't cry: he's always been the rock in our family, and he always says he's never shed a tear about the fact that I don't have arms.'

Later that day Bill was holding Jessica in his arms when a woman came up to him and said something that was to set the tenor for her whole life. 'She looked at my dad and she said, "you know what? You must be pretty special parents for God to bless you with a child like this one." Sometimes I wonder whether that woman was an angel. Certainly she was the voice of God in our lives; and because of her, my dad was able to see through the shock and chaos and to believe things would all be ok in the end.'

Growing up in the US state of Arizona, Jessica was surrounded by love and fun and by faith: her mother, Inez, is from the Philippines, her dad is American, and she was raised as Catholic. From the start, she says, they knew the most important thing they could do was simply to believe in her: their message was never about what she couldn't do, but always about what she could do. And, as it turned out, that was anything. Anything she set her mind to, anyway. So she learned to swim and dive, and from the top board at the swimming pool too. She enrolled for dancing classes, and when the time came for the annual performance in front of all the mums and dads, she knew she couldn't hide at the back, even though it was scary being the kid with no arms in the spotlight. She learned an important lesson that day, she says. 'It was a huge auditorium filled with people, and when the lights came on and the music began to play and we did the first bit of the dance, I heard a round of applause. A little bit of courage sparked in me. It was an affirmation: I realised I belonged. I wasn't supposed to stay hidden in the shadows; my place was here in the light, with the other girls.'

But a big problem for Jessica, in the first 11 years of her life, was her prosthetic arms. 'I hated them, because they slowed me down. They were heavy and they made me feel half-human, half-robot; and I could do everything more quickly without them, using my feet.' And so, when she started at secondary school, she made the big decision to stop using them. 'Going without my prosthetic arms made me feel proud, and free, and independent,' she says. 'It meant I had accepted myself for who I was, and that meant I was inviting other people to do the same. It made me authentic and comfortable in my own skin.'

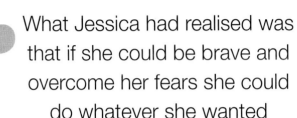

What Jessica had realised was that if she could be brave and overcome her fears she could do whatever she wanted

What Jessica had realised was that if she could be brave and overcome her fears she could do whatever she wanted. She developed an instinct for meeting challenges head-on by determining to beat them, and to prove the doubters around her wrong. Time and again in her childhood and adolescent years she was aware of people around her silently shaking their heads and saying to themselves, Jessica won't be able to do that. 'And every time, it only made me more determined to succeed,' she says. 'Their doubts spurred me on to do whatever it was they thought I couldn't do.'

All the same, when she decided to learn to fly it looked as though perhaps this time she had bitten off more than she could chew. 'There are no pilots in my family, and flying was my greatest fear; and that's when I realised it was something I had to conquer, to be true to myself,' she remembers. She was 21 years old at the time, and just out of college. She registered for flying lessons, found an instructor who believed in her, and learned to control the

> What I discovered was that, if you want something badly enough, you'll be able to figure a way to do it

plane with her feet. Just as she had all her life, whenever anyone doubted her it just propelled her on to try harder. 'One day someone said, we've tried everything we can to make you a pilot, I just don't think it's going to work,' she remembers. 'And that was the moment I knew I'd be able to do it.'

At the same time she was working out how to deal with her life, Jessica was realising that many of the things that were happening to her were metaphors for what happens to all of us. 'In a way everyone is born without arms, in the sense that we all have challenges,' she says. 'The thing about my challenges were that they're just more public than most. But not having arms is an emotional disability we all suffer from, each of us in our own way – and finding the courage to overcome whatever is stopping us from doing things is a life-giving force. What I discovered was that, if you want something badly enough, you'll be able to figure a way to do it.'

The first time she flew solo, remembers Jessica, something unexpected happened: her radio failed. 'It was a moment when I realised I was truly on my own: just me and God,' she says. 'I immediately knew what I had to do was to fly the aeroplane first, and everything was fine. But that experience made me aware of the place of faith in my life. I was flying that plane alone, but I wasn't alone. God was with me; and God has always been with me, and with my parents in helping them to help me.'

Today Jessica is a motivational speaker, and she travels all over the world with her husband Patrick, whom she married six years ago. From the first time they met, she says, he accepted her for the person she is: when they got married, she put a ring on his finger and he put an anklet on her foot. When they drive somewhere in the car he holds onto her foot the way people hold hands. 'We just adjusted our lives, and we get on with it,' she says. She's looking forward to being a mother, and when you ask if she finds the prospect daunting she says the same thing a million other young women might say: the prospect of all those sleepless nights scare her. But

God often works in mysterious ways, and you just have to be patient and trust him

the thought of how she'll cope with a baby given that she has no arms... well, the idea that it could be tough hasn't really occurred to her. Why should it? One of the most wonderful things about her life, she says, is that the way she's different brings out the best in people. We meet on a trip she's made to Europe on her own; at the airport, she says, a fellow traveller was desperate to help her. 'I knew I'd be quicker than him at getting my suitcase off the carousel, but I figured he really wanted to help so I thought I should let him,' she says.

And one day a few years ago, her mum came to hear her doing one of her motivational talks. 'She's always told me that, after I was born, she asked God why he made me the way he did. She just couldn't understand it. But God often works in mysterious ways, and you just have to be patient and trust him. Three decades on, my mum saw me on the stage, sharing my message about courage and resilience and never taking no for an answer with hundreds of people in the audience. She could see everyone listening very intently, and she knew what I was saying was making a difference. And that's when she understood that God had a purpose all along. All it takes is faith, and anything is possible.'

2

The mother who lost her son to violence – and who now spreads the word on peace

Margaret Mizen's 16-year-old son Jimmy died in a senseless murder: and she knew when she lost him that there was only one way forward.

Jimmy Mizen was feeling lucky: it was the day after his 16th birthday, and he decided to head to the local shops to buy a lottery ticket. A totally ordinary, everyday event: but one from which he would never return. Because on that day, 10 May 2008, Jimmy was murdered in a senseless stabbing after a row in a bakery near the family home in south east London.

That day changed everything for his mother Margaret and her husband Barry. It robbed them of seeing their child grow up, finish school, get a qualification, find a job. It stole from them the chance to see him get married and raise children of his own. Nothing will ever begin to fill the hole in their life, says Margaret: but, all the same, Jimmy's life is absolutely something to celebrate. 'We've always celebrated his life: even right after the

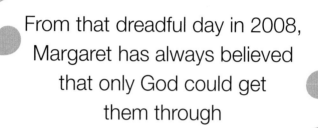

> From that dreadful day in 2008, Margaret has always believed that only God could get them through

funeral we had a party, and we all laughed together and told stories about Jimmy and remembered him. 'Of course there were lots of tears too – but I knew we had to celebrate, because it was a good life and he was a lovely boy.'

The Mizens, a strongly Catholic couple, have eight other children. Their survival as a family, explains Margaret when we meet, has been their faith.

From that dreadful day in 2008, Margaret has always believed that only God could get them through.

'Right from the earliest days, Barry and I were determined that we had to bring something good out of this, or it would destroy us,' she explains. 'We didn't want that to happen, so we prayed and prayed. We prayed especially in the middle of the night when we couldn't get to sleep for crying. We prayed for the strength and the grace to cope; we believed we could do that, we believed God would show us the path.'

Today Margaret believes God did show them the path. Within a few weeks of Jimmy's death, some young people had sent her a small amount of money; more trickled in. The Mizens realised they could use Jimmy's loss to help other young people. 'We thought we could raise money to buy a school a minibus – we'd ask them to call it a Jimmy bus in our son's memory,' remembers Margaret.

Five years on, that minibus has been bought many times over: and in addition, the family have set up the Jimmy Mizen Foundation, a charitable trust devoted to spreading the message of peace and forgiveness amongst young people. These days Margaret and Barry spend much of their time giving talks in schools and youth groups, telling their story and hoping that the young people who hear will learn from it, and not get pulled down the route that led to Jimmy's death. Their foundation raises money to support youth organisations and also helps youngsters with work experience. And it also runs a coffee shop, the Cafe of Good Hope, where Margaret and I are talking – as well as providing a meeting-point for the local community, the cafe also gives work experience opportunities for young people from the neighbourhood. Margaret has never met Jake Fahri, the man who murdered her son – but she thinks about him a lot.

Most of all she wonders what it was in his history that led him to be so angry and hate-filled that day. He was 19 at the time of the murder, just three years older than Jimmy; and when Jimmy pulled him up for rudely trying to push him out of the way in the baker's shop, it triggered an altercation that quickly escalated into a full-scale fight culminating in Fahri smashing a glass bowl over Jimmy's head, piercing his neck and severing vital blood vessels. Jimmy died a few moments later in the arms of one of his brothers, Tommy. At Fahri's trial the prosecuting barrister described how Fahri had reached for every available weapon with which to attack Jimmy and his brother. The whole attack, said the lawyer, had been 'three minutes of absolute madness' on Fahri's part.

> What Margaret hopes is that her story will make young people pause, and reflect, before they resort to violence

What Margaret hopes is that her story will make young people pause, and reflect, before they resort to violence. She also hopes they'll realise the power of God in their lives. 'When something like this happens to you, you find there are people who want someone or something to blame. They blame the perpetrator, they blame the circumstances or the police or the authorities, and most of all they blame God.

'But I never wanted to blame God, because I knew that only God would get me through,' says Margaret. 'There were days after Jimmy's death when I'd wake up and I didn't believe I'd be able to get out of bed. It would just seem like an impossible thing to do. And then I'd feel as though God was lifting my legs, one after the other, out of the bed and onto the floor. 'God carried me through.'

> What's extraordinary about the Mizen family is that none of them has ever sought revenge or retribution over Jimmy's death

What's extraordinary about the Mizen family is that none of them has ever sought revenge or retribution over Jimmy's death. 'Barry and I were very clear about that, right from the start,' says Margaret. 'And I'm very proud of the fact that all our sons have the same attitude. Jimmy had six brothers, and it would be very easy to imagine that young lads would want revenge over their brother's death in such terrible circumstances. But they've all followed our lead, they're all involved in the foundation or supportive of what it does, and I'm really proud of them for being behind us in our message of forgiveness and hope.'

More than a decade on from Jimmy's death, Margaret says her life has changed out of all recognition. Some of her children still live at home – including her daughter Samantha, who has Down's Syndrome – but, she says, she now lives a totally different life.

'I've been to places I never expected to go, like Kenya with CAFOD to look at the peace projects there,' she says. 'And I've met so many people I'd never have dreamed of meeting – Prince Charles, Boris Johnson, Archbishop Nichols. They've all been kind to us and supportive of what we're doing, and we're enormously grateful.

'Nothing will ever bring Jimmy back, and we understood that right from the start – but ten years on I'm proud of what we've done in his name, and know he'd be proud of it too.'

3

The fish farmer who feeds more than a million children each day

Magnus MacFarlane-Barrow had a simple ambition: to provide school lunches for children in developing countries. Working out of his garden shed in Scotland, he made it happen.

Just off the road to Oban, in an undulating, heather-strewn valley overlooked by the snow-dusted Ben Lui, stands a small, corrugated-iron shed that is making the difference between a life of misery and a life of opportunity – and sometimes even life and death – for more than a million children thousands of miles away.

The shed was the birthplace in 2002 of a tiny charity called Mary's Meals, and it is still its powerhouse today. Sitting in the shed, scrupulously modest about his achievements and in no doubt of the huge task that still lies ahead, is Magnus MacFarlane-Barrow, whom former Prime Minister Gordon Brown once described as a man who is following in the footsteps of other great Scottish missionary heroes such as David Livingstone and Eric Liddell of Chariots of Fire fame.

> These awful images were coming in, and it was clear there was great need – and I decided to fill my Land Rover with supplies and drive there to help

Apart from his mouthful of a name, there is nothing complicated about either Magnus or his approach to helping the world's disadvantaged. His experience as a charity worker began in the early 1990s during the Bosnian war. 'These awful images were coming in, and it was clear there was great need – and I decided to fill my Land Rover with supplies and drive there to help,' he says. At the time he was a fish farmer on the west coast of Scotland.

In 1983 his deeply Catholic family travelled to a Bosnian village called Medjugorje because of reports that some of its residents were seeing visions of the Virgin Mary. 'I was shocked by what was happening to the people there,' he says.

That first trip was followed by many more, and on one of them he gave a lift to a young nurse named Julie, who wanted to volunteer. A few years later they married – the couple now have seven children. Their family home is a few metres from the corrugated-iron shed that became Magnus's charity HQ. The shed had been his and his siblings' playroom when he was a boy, and when he needed somewhere from which to administer his Bosnian trips, it seemed a perfect makeshift office. The charity – then called Scottish International Relief – garnered a huge amount of public support, and towards the end of the 1990s Magnus travelled to Liberia, and then Malawi, with a view to extending the charity's reach to needy parts of Africa.

It was in a village in Malawi in 2002 that he had a conversation that was to change his life. 'I was staying with an Italian priest and he asked me if I wanted to go on his rounds with him. We went to this particular village because there was a mother dying of Aids, and she had six children. It was a desperate situation; she was saying that all she had left to hope for was that someone would care for her children after she had gone.'

Her eldest son, Edward, who was 14, was beside her and Magnus admits that it was more to try to find some shred of hope in the family's plight than for any other reason that he asked the boy what his dreams were. 'He said, "To have enough food to eat and to go to school." And with that, everything crystallised for me.'

What Magnus realised was that one simple intervention could transform life for Edward and children like him all over the developing world: the provision of a school dinner for them each day.

That conversation with Edward took place in November 2002; by January 2003 the first school meals were being set down in front of children who were used to having to do their lessons hungry.

'When we researched it, we found that many children were coming to school without having had any breakfast, and they weren't getting anything at school – so it would be evening before they got fed,' he says. 'We knew that changing that would make a difference.'

Today, Mary's Meals works in 17 countries across Africa, Asia, Latin America, Eastern Europe and the Caribbean, and feeds more than 1.3 million

> 61 million children across the world are out of school and hungry, and in the years ahead they're determined to feed more and more of those kids

children a day. But 61 million children across the world are out of school and hungry, and in the years ahead they're determined to feed more and more of those kids – and to give them the crucial opportunity to learn, and to have choices in their lives.

'You find that when school dinners are provided after the first year of introduction, enrolment increases by around 36% – in some instances school roll has doubled in a matter of weeks,' explains Magnus.

'In the short term that can be problematic, but in the long term it's fantastic. And attendance rates go up

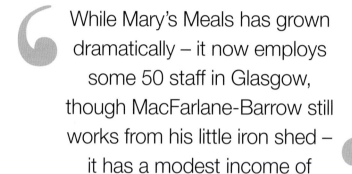

While Mary's Meals has grown dramatically – it now employs some 50 staff in Glasgow, though MacFarlane-Barrow still works from his little iron shed – it has a modest income of £15 million a year

too, because in many schools children are enrolled but don't attend school very often, and that changes once they know they will be fed. And academic performance also improves a lot – because now not only are children coming to school; they are also not hungry in lessons.'

The successes are all the more remarkable given how little it costs: £13.90 to feed a child for a whole school year. While Mary's Meals has grown dramatically – it now employs some 50 staff in

Glasgow, though MacFarlane-Barrow still works from his little iron shed – it has a modest income of £18 million a year.

Clearly a great deal is being done with comparatively little, and although some development thinkers have criticised the charity for its lack of sustainability, Magnus believes that, by existing outside the constraints of grants and government funding, Mary's Meals is able to take a longer-term view.

'We are not caught in three – or five-year funding cycles,' he says. 'We are a grassroots movement, with support from grassroots supporters, many of them schoolchildren here who want to support schoolchildren like them in other parts of the world.'

In 2012 one young supporter, nine-year-old Martha Payne from Lochgilphead, catapulted Mary's Meals to new heights of fame when she started a fundraising blog about her own school dinners and was briefly banned from doing so by her local council. 'I was in the US at the time, and I was a bit surprised to read about it in the New York Times,' says Magnus.

Last year, 12 years after their first meeting, MacFarlane-Barrow travelled to Malawi and saw Edward again. He describes their reunion as 'painful'. His big regret was that, although he had used Edward's words and sentiments to fuel his charity, he had not been able to make it work quickly enough for Edward himself.

> His big regret was that, although he had used Edward's words and sentiments to fuel his charity, he had not been able to make it work quickly enough for Edward himself

'For various reasons, Mary's Meals hadn't happened in his school, and I feel very sad about that,' he says. There is, though, a silver lining. Today Edward, who is 26, has a young son of his own. Now he's at school, he has a Mary's Meals dinner each day, and Magnus takes comfort from that.

4

The nun with fire in her soul

Helen Prejean became famous across the world when Susan Sarandon won an Oscar for playing her on screen in the movie Dead Man Walking. Three decades on, she's still battling for an end to capital punishment.

The defining moment in Sister Helen Prejean's life came just after midnight on 5 April 1984 when she watched a man die. She had spent the whole of the last day of his life with him, and both of them knew that his end was near. But despite the inevitability of it, she says, she could never come to terms with how it ended. 'What I saw that night set my soul on fire,' she says today. 'And it's a fire that burns in me still.'

The man who Sister Helen saw die was called Patrick Sonnier; and though he knew he was going to die that night, he was an entirely healthy 34-year-old. He died because he had been condemned to death by a US court after being convicted of murder; Sister Helen, who was his spiritual advisor, was the last person allowed to be with him. She walked with

 That night she promised God and Patrick Sonnier that she'd spread the word about how abhorrent capital punishment was, and how it could not be allowed to continue in a world that wanted to call itself civilised

him to the execution chamber, with her hand on his shoulder, reciting psalms; and just before he died, he looked into her face in what she knows was a gesture of love and gratitude to her for being his friend.

After they'd pronounced him dead, Sister Helen says she went outside to the car park and threw up:

she simply couldn't believe the inhumanity she'd witnessed. And that night she promised God and Patrick Sonnier that she'd spread the word about how abhorrent capital punishment was, and how it could not be allowed to continue in a world that wanted to call itself civilised.

The result of that promise was a book called Dead Man Walking, which was published 20 years ago and became an instant bestseller. In 1995 it became a movie directed by Tim Robbins, and his wife Susan Sarandon played the role of Sister Helen and received an Oscar for her performance.

But the campaign didn't end there for Sister Helen: more than three decades after the death of Sonnier, she is still touring the globe opposing capital punishment. She's feisty, straight-talking and fun; she talks in a low, deep Southern drawl, laughs a lot, and is a fabulous storyteller, which is, of course, why Dead Man Walking had such extraordinary success as a movie, and has touched so many. One of her many stories is typically self-deprecating: she tells me that when Tim Robbins first heard his story, he pronounced his verdict. 'He said, "the nun was in over her head",' she says, laughing at the memory.

'And I was. I had no idea how to handle what was happening to me. I made plenty of mistakes.'

We meet during a trip she's making to London, where she's giving a speech in which she'll argue that capital punishment, as well as being inhumane, doesn't actually work: in the 31 American states that retain the death penalty, she points out, murder rates are consistently higher than in the 19 without.

It's hard to believe, when you're face to face with Sister Helen, that she's now in her late seventies. She jokes self-deprecatingly about how she's not a bit like Susan Sarandon – 'she was a dead ringer, wasn't she?' – but the truth is she looks much younger than her years. It's not just her looks, it's her passion too: none of the fire, as she says, has gone out. 'I made a promise to Pat, and I've never forgotten that promise,' she says.

And the promise has paid off. Sister Helen is too modest to claim it as her victory, but the fact is that through her long years of campaigning, and despite the fact that there are still hundreds of prisoners on death row across the US, there have been many significant steps forward. 'Things are getting a lot better in the US,' she says. 'In 2000 there were 231 death sentences handed down, in 2012, there were only 77. The number of executions is down too; and more states are getting rid of the death penalty, or moving towards it.'

> I made a promise to Pat, and I've never forgotten that promise

What Sister Helen, as a Catholic nun, is especially pleased about is that the views of members of her own church in the US have changed considerably over recent years. 'American Catholics have shifted more than any other faith group,' she says. 'They're now at below the national average in terms of their support for the death penalty – one third of them have shifted from being in favour, to being against.'

What's more, says Sister Helen, a survey in 1987 found that the more often people went to church, the more they were for the death penalty. Today that is reversed: the more frequent a churchgoer someone is, the less likely he or she is to be in favour of the death penalty.

That can hardly fail to be linked to the fact that Pope St John Paul II became more vociferous in his opposition to capital punishment during his pontificate; and that was undoubtedly due at least in part to 'Dead Man Walking', which he watched, and to meeting and speaking with Sister Helen.

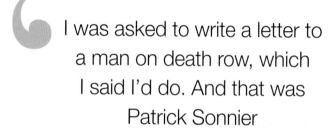

> I was asked to write a letter to a man on death row, which I said I'd do. And that was Patrick Sonnier

'We had a direct dialogue,' she remembers. 'My question to him was: our Church is pro-life, but why does the Catholic Church only uphold the dignity of innocent life?' More recently, Pope Francis has delighted Sister Helen by changing the Catechism to say the death penalty is no longer admissible under any circumstances, because 'it is an attack on the inviolability and dignity of the person'.

'When I'm walking with a man to his execution, he's been rendered totally hopeless,' says Sister Helen. 'And he's saying to me, please God hold up my legs so I can make it into the execution chamber.' The Catechism, she says, had already stated the dignity of innocent life: but what Pope Francis's changes mean is that it now says that even those who have done terrible crimes have an inviolable dignity. 'And part of that dignity is not to be strapped down and rendered defenceless and killed by an intentional act. That's what changed in this. No exceptions.'

These days Sister Helen is one of the biggest experts on the death penalty in the world: but things were very different back in the early 1980s. She'd joined her convent, the Congregation of St Joseph, at the age of 18 in her native Louisiana. At first, she says, she worked in 'a nice area'; but then came Vatican II, and the call to reach out to the poor. 'I'd never met any poor people, but I decided I'd go to work with them in New Orleans. And while I was there I was asked to write a letter to a man on death row, which I said I'd do. And that was Patrick Sonnier; and when he asked me to visit, I said I would. And then everything snowballed from there.'

But being a champion for the abolition of the death penalty has brought Sister Helen much criticism as well as much praise. Some of it, she says humbly, is down to her own failings: she now regrets, she says, that she didn't go to visit the families of the two young people who Patrick Sonnier and his brother murdered. 'The strange thing in this story is that everyone was Catholic,' she says. 'The Sonniers were Catholics, and the two teenagers who they killed were also from Catholic families.' So when a

> I still am, and I always will be, profoundly shocked by the taking of human life in this way. It's unspeakable. It has to stop

religious sister became one of the leading advocates for the condemned criminal, it more than rankled with the families. 'I made a huge mistake: I knew that losing your child was every parent's nightmare, and I avoided going to see them because I was scared. I thought they'd be angry at me because I was the spiritual advisor to the man who killed their children.

'But the truth is that whenever I meet a family who have lost a loved one, I feel guilty. Because although I know the death penalty is wrong, I haven't suffered as they have. But ultimately I know that the execution is a deceptive source of peace for them: they think it will bring them closure and justice, but it won't.'

So now, says Sister Helen, she works with victims' families as well as with prisoners on death row. She's not been present at an execution since 2000 – after Patrick Sonnier, there were five more inmates who she accompanied to their deaths – but, she says, if one of those she's currently supporting ended up in the electric chair, she wouldn't flinch from being there by his or her side. 'It's not something that ever gets any easier,' she says. 'Each time is exactly like the first.

'I still am, and I always will be, profoundly shocked by the taking of human life in this way. It's unspeakable. It has to stop.'

5

The couple who survived death row

Sunny Jacobs and Peter Pringle are a married couple with a unique common bond – both were wrongly convicted of capital offences, and both spent time on death row. Today they're putting their experiences to use in helping others who've been exonerated after being convicted of crimes they didn't commit.

In 1998 Sunny Jacobs, who had spent 17 years on death row in the US before being exonerated of the crime for which she was convicted, was invited to speak at an Amnesty International meeting in Ireland. Before she left, an activist friend remarked that, if she was going to the west of Ireland, she really ought to meet Peter Pringle; but he didn't say why.

Fast forward a few weeks, and there was Sunny on a podium in Galway, speaking about her wrongful conviction and her long years in jail when she lived in daily dread of the steps on the corridor that would herald the news that she'd been given an execution date. And on the front row was a man who, it was obvious to Sunny, was deeply moved by her testimony.

> Fifteen years on from their first meeting, I am having lunch with Sunny and Peter in the town where they first met, Galway

'I could see how upset this guy was becoming, and out of concern for him I actually toned my talk down,' she remembers. 'I really didn't want him to be so upset.'

At the end of Sunny's presentation, the man approached her to talk more about her story. Later he offered to drive her to her next stop, which was in Cork. 'And it was only on the journey that I got round to saying, so what's your interest in all this?' says Sunny. 'And when he told me, I could hardly believe what I was hearing.'

The man was Peter Pringle, one of the last people ever to be sentenced to death in Ireland. Like Sunny, he had spent many years of his life on death row; he was convicted in 1980, and capital punishment was only officially abolished there ten years later. Like Sunny, he had eventually been released and cleared of the crime for which he was convicted; and like Sunny, he now devoted much of his life to campaigning against the death penalty and to speaking out for victims of miscarriages of justice.

Fifteen years on from their first meeting, I am having lunch with Sunny and Peter in the town where they first met, Galway. They could be any regular later-life couple: they both listen patiently, and then a little impatiently, to one another's stories. They finish one another's sentences, and Peter at 75, 11 years older than Sunny helps her collect her lunch and carries it over to the table, because Sunny has a chronic back problem that makes walking difficult.

Galway is their home now and, astonishingly, Sunny and Peter really are a married couple. In fact, says Peter, they got married twice: once in a private ceremony down on the beach for just the two of them, on the day of the winter solstice ('there was the sun in one direction, and the moon in the other,' remembers Sunny); and the second time in New York, where actor Brooke Shields who played Sunny in a play about death row prisoners who were later proved innocent was one of the guests.

Talking to them, you realise they're very different characters with very different backgrounds: Sunny was raised in a Jewish family in New York, Peter grew up a Catholic in Ireland. But what unites them is an experience each considered unique before they met the other: neither had ever expected to have such a close relationship with anyone else who had known how it feels to be innocent, and yet facing the death penalty. Bizarrely, the crimes for which they were convicted were almost identical: Sunny was tried for the murder of two police officers, Peter for the murder of two members of the Irish garda.

Today, Peter says he has identified four basic elements that were features of both his case and Sunny's, and are probably often there in a case of wrongful conviction. 'In both our cases there was false testimony; there was prosecutorial misconduct; a false witness was used, and there was a deal done whereby someone on a lesser charge was promised the allegations against them would be dropped if they gave evidence against the main defendants. The fact is that, especially in a case where police officers have been killed, the investigating officials are under enormous pressure to come up with a defendant,' says Peter. 'Everyone wants results. Not justice, note: results. So if they realise they can move things round

Peter remembers one police officer telling him: 'I actually believe you didn't do this, but my bosses really want to pin it on you which suggests to me that you must have done something

a bit, make the allegations stick, they often take that route.' Peter remembers one police officer telling him: 'I actually believe you didn't do this, but my bosses really want to pin it on you which suggests to me that you must have done something.'

At their very first meeting in 1998, the couple realised how drawn they were to one another; but it wasn't until 2001, when Sunny was again visiting Ireland and ended up stranded there by the lack of flights after 9/11, that she and Peter realised there was a romantic connection. They pondered whether to base themselves in California, where Sunny was living, or in Ireland; and the simplicity of the lifestyle there, says Sunny, made Ireland the winner. 'I gave all

> 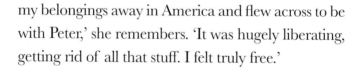 Coming to terms with the loss of so much of her life has, she admits, been very tough

my belongings away in America and flew across to be with Peter,' she remembers. 'It was hugely liberating, getting rid of all that stuff. I felt truly free.'

And freedom is all the more cherished by those who have gone without it, especially those like Sunny and Peter who have gone without it unjustly. In Sunny's case, there was the additional trauma of having to cope with the fact that her then boyfriend and co-defendant, Jesse Tafero, with whom she had been travelling on the day two policemen stopped their car and were killed, was executed in horrific circumstances (the electric chair malfunctioned, and it took 13.5 minutes for him to die). Only after his death did the other person who was with them on the day of the murders confess that it was him, and not Jesse or Sunny, who fired the fatal shots. At the age of 45, Sunny was released after 17 years in jail but into a very different world. Her children (including a daughter, Christina, who had been ten months old at the time of her imprisonment) were grown up. Coming to terms with the loss of so much of her life has, she admits, been very tough.

And as for Sunny, so too for Peter. He was arrested after two police officers, Henry Byrne and John Morley, were shot in Loughglynn, County Roscommon in the aftermath of a bank robbery. The men fleeing the scene were masked and Peter, who was arrested a fortnight after the deaths, always denied having anything to do with it; but it wasn't until 1995, after he had served 15 years and had had to listen to his jailers talking about how he'd be executed, that his conviction was finally overturned.

When they met, Peter and Sunny discovered that, as well as the circumstances of their convictions being so alike, they had also both coped with prison in remarkably similar ways. 'When we talked we realised that, for both of us, yoga and meditation had been fundamental to our survival,' says Sunny. 'The thing our stories show is that everyone has the potential inside themselves to deal with terrible things,' says Peter. 'We all have to deal with trauma at some point in our lives, and at some stage something will come along that will seem unsurmountable. But I believe God never gives us anything to suffer that we can't

 Our story gives everyone hope

deal with; the trick is to go inside yourself and find out what you have got to help you deal with what you're up against. People don't realise that they have the capacity within themselves to heal themselves.'

Perhaps because they both lost so much of their lives to prison, Peter and Sunny though now aged 75 and 66 have ambitious plans for the future. Having found happiness themselves despite all they've been through, they're determined to do what they can to help others in a similar situation; and they're hoping to set up a retreat centre for prisoners who, like them, have been exonerated after a long period of imprisonment. 'We want to establish a place where people who are released can come to decompress, where they can be part of a living family as they start to recover from what they've been through,' says Peter. 'You can't just go straight back into normal life after an experience like that; you need to feel safe, you need to be with people who understand, and you need the help of healing professionals. We'd like to have a house big enough to have a yoga workshop and perhaps an arts studio, and animals and a garden, a beautiful place where people who had been through so much could start to feel properly alive again.'

Beyond that, though, they feel their story should give heart to anyone in the world, whatever they're up against and however bleak the outlook seems. 'Our story gives everyone hope,' says Peter. 'If you can go through everything we've gone through, and meet as late in life as we did, and find the truly great happiness we've now found... well, there's hope for everyone.'

6

The mother whose son committed an atrocity

Terri Roberts could hardly believe what her son had been responsible for: but against all the odds, she used it to give witness to her Christian faith and the power of forgiveness.

Terri Roberts was at the theatre where she worked when the call came. It was her husband, Chuck. Terri should come straight away, he said, to their son Charlie's house. Terri knew instantly, from the tone of Chuck's voice, that it was serious. She didn't ask questions, just ran to her car. And it was on the short drive that she turned on the radio and heard for the first time about a shooting incident that morning at a school in a nearby town.

Several children were dead, the report said, and the perpetrator was a man named Roy. Terri suspected immediately that the killings were connected with Chuck's call. 'I knew straight away that the school they were talking about was very near the place

> She remembers the initial disbelief, the feeling that it was utterly impossible that her lovely son, her quiet, deep, complicated but loving son, who had three young children of his own, could possibly be responsible for such an unthinkable tragedy

where our son Charlie used to park the milk van he drove,' she says. 'I was imagining all sorts of dreadful things, like that he had been killed while helping to rescue some of the children. I knew he'd have helped them if he possibly could.'

Terri thought she was imagining the worst: in fact, the worst would turn out to be infinitely more appalling. When she arrived at Charlie's house the

first people she saw in the driveway were Chuck
and a police officer. She remembers what happened
next as if it was in slow motion.

'I said to the officer, "Is my son still alive?"
He said 'no'.

'Then I turned to Chuck, whose eyes were sunk deep
into his face, and he said to me: "It was Charlie. He
killed those children."'

The next few hours were a blur to Terri. She
remembers the initial disbelief, the feeling that
it was utterly impossible that her lovely son, her
quiet, deep, complicated but loving son, who had
three young children of his own, could possibly be
responsible for such an unthinkable tragedy. Hadn't
she heard the name Roy on the radio? And then, as
it gradually dawned on her that what Chuck had
told her must somehow be true, and that the Roy
mentioned on the radio had simply been a mistake,
she remembers falling to the floor and lying there in
a foetal position, and howling. Just howling.

In many ways, the most extraordinary part of
Terri's story is that she ever managed to get up

off that floor and didn't spend the rest of her life just lying there howling. Because the details of the slaughter for which her son was responsible for are hard to write, hard to read and almost impossible to imagine or to begin to understand.

Here are the facts: on the morning of 2 October 2006, Charlie Roberts, carrying a gun, walked into the classroom of an Amish school near his home in Pennsylvania. He ordered the boys to leave and, half an hour later, shot 10 of the girls before turning the gun on himself. Five died: the youngest two were seven, the oldest was 12. Two of them, Lena and Mary Liz Miller, aged eight and seven respectively, were sisters. Five more girls were injured, including six-year-old Rosanna King who was initially not expected to survive and who has severe brain injuries.

How do you begin to understand that your child has been responsible for a tragedy of this magnitude? Like Eva Khatchadourian, the mother of the killer in Lionel Shriver's novel *We Need to Talk about Kevin*, Terri has combed through every detail, every nuance, every memory, every clue, to try to work out what in her eldest son's past could have made him walk into that schoolhouse that day. 'What did I miss?' she asks. 'I was – always will be – his mother. Surely if anyone could spot signs of trouble it would be the woman who gave birth to him. At what point did bitterness begin to seethe beneath the surface contentment? Or hate tug harder at the mind and heart than love?'

 ## As a mother, she says, she cannot stop loving her son

As a mother, she says, she cannot stop loving her son – and as she unravels his story – the ordinary story of an ordinary boy in an ordinary town whose life ended so violently – you feel she is doing what any parent can and must do, even in the face of odds as great as these, which is to see the very best in her child, to give him the benefit of every doubt, to put every tale in the most sympathetic light. Yet, when she has finished describing how sweet a baby he was, and how he had to cope with being born with club feet, and his learning difficulties, and the loss of his first child soon after her birth, the question hangs in the air between us, and Terri is brave enough, through her tears, to name it and answer it herself. 'I ask myself, were these things related to what happened? But the truth is that plenty of people in the world have experienced extreme pain and suffering, and have coped with it. They didn't go on to commit terrible crimes like Charlie did.'

> If you have a child who is quiet and reserved, especially when hard things happen, it's worth reflecting with them to see if there's anything deep that needs to come to the surface

After the murders, a note was found in which Charlie confessed to having sexually assaulted two young female relatives 20 years earlier and said he was still haunted by it. Yet, says Terri, police investigations never found any evidence that what he had confessed to had, in fact, happened.

Looking back, she remembered Charlie was always quiet as a boy. 'But I have a husband who is quiet and another son who is quiet. It's not unusual for men to be quiet.'

Could there really have been no sign that Charlie was disturbed at a very deep level? Terri is adamant that there were not. 'After it happened, I got together with his best friend and we talked. He said, "I never saw anything in Charlie that would have brought him to anger or resentment. It just wasn't there…" The only thing I can say is, he obviously masked hurt deeper than I could ever have imagined. So yes, as a mother I wish – how much I wish – I had drawn him out more. If I have any message for other mothers, it's this: if you have a child who is quiet and reserved, especially when hard things happen, it's worth reflecting with them to see if there's anything deep that needs to come to the surface.'

The truth is, and Terri knows it, that whatever terrible things were going on inside Charlie, they were probably too deeply buried for anyone else to access. 'Somewhere in my son's life he experienced some kind of pain that he internalised and never shared with anyone. He internalised something so painful that it opened up a door for evil. Something grabbed hold of him that was so dark and so deep.'

Terri is a Christian – she raised Charlie as a Christian – but since the tragedy she has had some big questions. 'I've said to God, I simply don't understand how you could let it happen. You could have given his car a flat tyre. In the end, I've had to admit that there can be no understanding. I've chosen to trust God because there's nothing else I can do. I have no understanding of why.'

Of course, there have been times when she has burned with anger at Charlie. How could he have done this? 'How could he... leave his wife a widow, his children fatherless? Leave them to face the shame and the horror? And the gentle Amish families he had come to know so well in his rounds collecting milk. What darkness and evil could so possess his mind that he would want to hurt them? To rip away daughters as precious as his own? To inflict such pain and loss on another living soul?'

After the shooting, and especially in the early days afterwards, Terri was acutely aware of how she, as Charlie's mother, and the whole of their family, was being judged and seen by others. 'It was scary,' she says. 'Knowing we were being labelled. In some ways it was harder for Chuck than for me – he's a retired police officer. He even has the same name as Charlie, so when he was showing his driving licence or something, people would do a double take and he'd have to say, "Yes, that's right, I'm the father".'

> **Something truly extraordinary happened – something that injects a glimmer of hope and faith and goodness into a story that is otherwise laced with horror and heartache**

Even going out shopping, or anywhere in public, meant they would be looked at, pointed at, blamed. Then something truly extraordinary happened – something that injects a glimmer of hope and faith and goodness into a story that is otherwise laced with horror and heartache.

Charlie's funeral was difficult for his parents and his wife, Marie, to organise: what undertaker, after all, would want to handle the burial of a man so loathed? Eventually, though, it was arranged. The family braced themselves for a media barrage. As they walked through the churchyard, Terri remembers, she could see the telescopic lenses trained on them. 'We felt vulnerable – we knew everyone was looking at us. Then, from behind a shed, a group of Amish people appeared, men in tall hats and women in white bonnets. They fanned out into a line between the graveside and the road. They were protecting us from the media.'

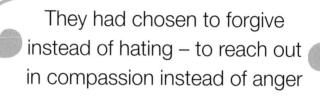

They had chosen to forgive instead of hating – to reach out in compassion instead of anger

There was more. 'When the service ended, these people came forward, these lovely people whose eyes, like mine, were red with tears. The first ones to approach us were Chris and Rachel Miller, whose daughters Lena and Mary Liz had both died in their arms. And they said to me: "We are so sorry for your loss."'

'There are no words to describe what it feels like when people who have suffered so much at the hands of your son reach out and say something like that', says Terri. 'It was an amazing thing to know that through their suffering they wanted to comfort us.'

Forgiveness, she says, is a choice. 'These sweet parents were still as grief-stricken as I was, their hearts broken like mine over the loss of their children. But they had chosen to forgive instead of hating – to reach out in compassion instead of anger.'

As time went by, there were further opportunities for Terri to connect with the Amish community and one day a chance came to visit Rosanna, the little girl who had pulled through, but with brain damage.

'I felt a need, a motherly need I guess, to connect. It was about two months afterwards, and I was invited to the house. They welcomed me in and gave me a seat next to Rosanna who was there in her wheelchair. She was so sweet and she had been so disabled; it was quite an emotional experience. I managed to hold myself together while I was there, but when we left I just started to bawl. To know that my son was responsible for this…'

There were more visits to Rosanna's family and eventually something even more incredible happened. Terri noticed that the family – who also had three young sons – found it difficult to eat together because someone had to be with Rosanna, so she asked whether she could help by looking after her while the family ate. For several years she went once a week and, these days, still visits regularly, even though she is no longer in good health. 'I had breast cancer some years ago and now it's in my lungs,' she says.

She will go on visiting Rosanna, now 16, for as long as she can. 'She is very dear to my heart,' says Terri. 'She's become almost like a granddaughter.'

In the end, she says, there are no words to describe what happened, just as there is no explanation. But if the shooting in the Amish school that day represented the unthinkable, then what has taken place since seems to represent what might perhaps merit being called a miracle.

Terri Roberts has died since this interview was first published. Thanks to her family for permission to include it, and her inspiring story, in this book.

Charlie as a child

7

The naval officer who realised how much we could all learn from people with disabilities

Jean Vanier's organisation L'Arche has transformed the lives of many thousands of people, both with and without disabilities, across the world.

The live nativity at Christmas midnight Mass at the L'Arche community has something different about it: Mary, Joseph and the shepherds are all played by people with disabilities. It's entirely in character with a place that sums up, and lives out, what it means to treat those who are handicapped as equals, and to see them not as people who need looking after, but as individuals with a great deal to teach the rest of us.

L'Arche, which lies in a sleepy French village in the middle of a forest, was founded by a Canadian called Jean Vanier, who set it up after feeling appalled by the way he saw disabled people being treated in institutions. He's now 90, and has spent more than half a century championing the idea

> The truth is that each person is a treasure, and in discovering the treasure in others we discover it in ourselves, too

that the secret to happiness is to learn from those who are physically and intellectually challenged, to concentrate on what we can do rather than on what we can't, and – quite simply – to enjoy our time on earth.

There are a lot of people to accommodate at the Christmas Mass at L'Arche, because the community now numbers more than 200 people, out of a village population of around 2000. And this village, Trosly-Breuil, while still the heart of the L'Arche movement, is now but a small part of it: there are 150 more communities, in countries as far-flung as

Japan, Poland and Brazil, which adds up to many thousands of individuals, physically challenged and able-bodied, whose lives have been influenced, and often transformed, by the movement Vanier started.

It was back in 1964 when he first came to this village, which is a few kilometres outside the town of Compiègne in Picardy. An ex-naval officer who was searching for something meaningful to do with his life, he was invited to the village by a priest friend who lived here. But it was when he accompanied the priest to the institution where people with handicaps were looked after that Vanier realised this was his life's work: the patients were badly treated, dehumanised, and not seen as the individuals they so clearly were. 'They were condemned to a lesser life,' says Vanier. 'But the truth is that each person is a treasure, and in discovering the treasure in others we discover it in ourselves, too.' The first L'Arche community was born when Vanier took two young men from the institution to live with him in a house in the village: in a family-like setting they flourished, and Vanier's life was also deeply enhanced. 'We are transformed by living with people who are different and who have been humiliated,' he explains. 'The great pain of our world is that it is obsessed with competition and the need to win. But if you go down the ladder rather than up, you find people who are interested not in wealth and success but only in relationships – and you discover that is the secret to great happiness.'

Rooted in Christianity – although those who work for it come from all faiths and none – L'Arche has always been counter-cultural, but in today's world it seems to stand out more strikingly than ever. Does Vanier, tall and sprightly for his years, feel worried about the effect of the Trump era on the philosophy he has spent a lifetime trying to spread? Predictably enough, the ever-optimistic Vanier is still hopeful, even though he concedes that 'Donald Trump is the perfect example of the person I wish to change. But even though he says he doesn't want migrants and seems to be turning away the very people I say we could all learn so much from, still we are in a world where, thanks to information technology, people are talking to one another more than ever before. And I believe that is where hope lies. We also have to pay heed to what's going on: Trump is a cry for something, and that's what we have to listen to.'

He also has hope in today's young. 'Many of

them come to work in L'Arche, and what I see are ferocious individuals who want to learn how to live together. They're interested in how to make the planet more beautiful, and in working out how we can all be together. The young people are different from the generation before, and that gives me a lot

The L'Arche community in Trosly-Breuil depends on many youngsters who have volunteered to spend part of their lives alongside people with disabilities

of hope.' The L'Arche community in Trosly-Breuil depends on many youngsters who have volunteered to spend part of their lives alongside people with disabilities: the partnership between the young and the handicapped is one of the movement's many strengths.

Fittingly enough, happiness seems to radiate out of Vanier, and his favourite word is 'super' (Pope Francis is 'a super person, an amazing man', and you get the absolute sense with him that everyone is 'precious'); but the one time his smile fades is when I ask him how it feels to be the Catholic Church's most pre-eminent living saint. Like Mother Teresa, who was his friend, many expect him to be fast-tracked to sainthood when he dies: how does it feel, to have that sort of accolade? He shakes his head and looks, for the first time, a little sad. 'The problem is

Doing this work hasn't been a hardship: I've had fun, we have fun together. I've had the most marvellous time

that when people talk about me being a saint, they aren't thinking about what they should be doing, who they should be helping,' he says. 'Talking of me as a saint suggests I'm doing something other people can't do, which is the exact opposite of what I want to suggest. Everyone can do what I'm doing, which is to welcome the disadvantaged into their lives and to realise we have much to learn from them. Doing this work hasn't been a hardship: I've had fun, we have fun together. I've had the most marvellous time.'

Being with Vanier feels like being with someone who's very close to God; but it's only later in the day, when I'm invited to have supper in one of the L'Arche houses, that I start to properly understand what his contribution to caring for the disabled, those with both physical and learning difficulties, is really all about. Life at L'Arche is modelled on family life: disabled people and carers, known as assistants, live in houses that are as close as possible to ordinary homes. There are grab rails and wide corridors for the wheelchairs, but the sitting-room looks like an ordinary family sitting-room, with a large TV, sofas, armchairs and a rug. The house I'm in is home to seven people with disabilities and four assistants; in an ideal world, explains Gail, one of their number, there would be six carers.

Supper is served around a huge table: four of the residents are in wheelchairs, and three are severely disabled. What's immediately striking is how the disabled people are at the heart of the meal and the conversation: they're as much participants as the assistants and the less disabled residents. Everyone helps everyone else: one resident helps his neighbour with his spoon, another offers hers a drinking cup from time to time. The vegetables are served by Amelie: it takes her a bit longer to negotiate the spoon and to ladle the leeks in cheese sauce onto the plates, but time is not of the essence here, and enabling people to contribute is.

> At L'Arche sharing is a two-way street – and paying attention to those who seem to have least turns the world round, in an entirely positive and joyful way

There's no sense of exclusion around the table at L'Arche: being unable to communicate verbally doesn't mean being unable to communicate in other ways, and it's clear there are some big personalities among the residents. The three-course meal goes on for more than an hour, and involves a fair amount of mess: but mess, as Vanier would say, is part of the reality of life, and there's no attempt made to sanitise or prettify the proceedings. One resident, who clearly loves his pureed spinach, ends up with it all over his face, neck and hands; but he's clearly relished every minute of eating it – and everyone else has enjoyed sharing in how much he's enjoyed it, too. At L'Arche sharing is a two-way street – and paying attention to those who seem to have least turns the world round, in an entirely positive and joyful way.

Jean Vanier with resident

8

The man who lost his mother to sainthood

Pierluigi Molla's mother went to give birth, and never returned. Decades later, he saw her canonised in Rome.

The last time Pierluigi Molla saw his mother, she was leaving the family home to give birth to his youngest sister. It was April 1962; he remembers her final hug. 'She embraced all of us, and she held each of us very tight before she went out through the door,' he says. His mother, Gianna, was hoping and praying that, in a few days' time, she would be returning home with her new baby. But she already knew that there was a chance she would not be back.

Earlier in her pregnancy, Gianna – already the mother of three young children, and working as a doctor in

Milan – discovered she had a medical complication, a fibroid in her uterus, that was likely to cause problems at her baby's birth. Doctors gave her the option of having a hysterectomy, which would solve the problem but also end her baby's life and remove the possibility of further children; an abortion; or

> # No-one can replace a mother's love in a young child's life; Pierluigi, like all children who have experienced that loss, is in no doubt about that

an operation to remove the fibroid which was risky, and would mean there might still be problems at the birth, but which would save the baby's life. Gianna didn't hesitate in making her decision: she would have the operation to remove the fibroid, and she would hope and pray that all would be well at the delivery.

It wasn't. The baby – a girl named Gianna Emanuela after her mother – was born safely, but Gianna developed an infection. Seven days later she died, leaving her husband Pietro with not only the newborn but Pierluigi, then six, Mariolina, five, and Laura, three. On her deathbed, she said leaving her children was an unbelievably hard thing to do.

Fifty four years later, Pierluigi, now 61 and a successful businessman in Milan, is telling me about his mother; and though so much time has passed, it is clear how deeply affected he still is by her memory. She was, he says, such a loving and caring mother; more than anything, he remembers what it felt like to be looked after by her. 'I remember one day when we were skiing – she loved skiing – it started to rain, and she tried to shelter me so I wouldn't get wet,' he says. 'And I remember going out with her in her little Fiat when she went to visit her patients.'

No-one can replace a mother's love in a young child's life; Pierluigi, like all children who have experienced that loss, is in no doubt about that. But what happened after Gianna's death was truly remarkable, and unprecedented in the history of the Catholic Church: because Pierluigi's mother, the woman who put her own life on the line to save her child, was made a saint.

In 2004, Pierluigi and his surviving siblings (Mariolina

died as a child) were in St Peter's Square when Pope John Paul II officiated at her canonisation. 'Seeing the huge picture of my mother holding me as a baby hanging there in St Peter's was truly surreal,' he says. It was the first time that an individual had been canonised in the presence of his or her offspring. 'It was wonderful for us that my father, who has since died, was still alive – it meant a lot to our family that we were altogether on that day,' says Pierluigi.

What Pierlugi remembers first about the time after Gianna's death, apart from the sadness, is the upheaval. 'They brought her home in the night to die, and she took her last breath early in the morning,' he says. 'I remember seeing her lying on the table later that day, and people coming to the house to pay their respects.' His grandmother moved in to help his father care for the children, and one of his father's sisters, who was a nun and boarding school head, offered to take him and Mariolina as pupils. They went – Mariolina was only four at the time, and she died two years later of a complication after contracting measles.

Through his adolescence, says Pierluigi, his mother's presence was always there. 'We were a close family, and much loved, but my mother's spirit was never far away,' he says. And then, when he was about 14 or 15, he began to be aware that it wasn't only inside his family that his mother's memory, and her story, were cherished: people he didn't even know were becoming fascinated by what had happened

We were a close family, and much loved, but my mother's spirit was never far away

to Gianna Molla, and were interested in putting her case forward to the Vatican for beatification. 'This was the aftermath of Vatican II, and the Church was actively looking for examples of laypeople who had lived good and holy lives,' he says.

Through the 1970s, as he went through the normal rites of passage of teenage life – riding a motorbike, developing a liking for beer – the backdrop to his life was that priests and nuns and laypeople were campaigning for his mother's cause. 'We were involved with it, but my father worked very hard to make sure it didn't affect us too much – he didn't want it to take too much of a toll on our lives.' In time Pierluigi himself married, to Lisi, and they had a daughter, Ortensia; and it was only at this point in his life, he says, that he truly understood his mother's sacrifice.

'When I was a little boy I couldn't understand why my mother had done this, why she had taken a risk that might involve her having to leave us when we were still so young,' he says. 'But when I had my own child, I could imagine why she did what she did. She wanted my sister to have a life, so she gave her life so that would be possible; and as a parent, I could understand at last why she did that.'

His sister Gianna, he says, has devoted her life to the memory of their mother, and to caring for their father as he got older. 'I think she felt that as my mother sacrificed her life for her, so she would give her life to our mother's memory and to caring for our father, as she knew our mother would have wanted her to do,' he says. Gianna, like her mother, is a doctor. What's most strange for Pierluigi and his sisters, he says, is the idea that their mother is a canonised saint of the Church. 'We think of saints as people who are far from reality, people who lived long ago and lived lives very different from our own,' he says. 'But my mother was a real person to us, someone who did very ordinary things, who made our meals and who tidied up after us and who did her work as a doctor.

'What I hope is that she is remembered as the very real person she was; before we were born, for example, she used to go round town on a motorbike, and as a child I remember how she liked to drive quite fast in her car. She loved skiing and she loved walking – she was someone who really enjoyed the outdoors.

'We were a very ordinary, middle-class family, and my mother was the heart of that family and the centre of all our lives. Now we share her with everyone else – with the whole Church and with people who pray to her and love her, though in a slightly different way from the way we did. It's strange that part of our family history has become part of Church history – but we are enormously proud of her. We wish we hadn't had to lose her when we did, but it's wonderful that she now has a place in so many hearts around the world.'

9

The catholic priest who opened his church to his city's homeless

Fr Angel Garcia's idea was a simple one: to welcome those without shelter into the house of God.

On Calle Hortaleza in central Madrid a blue neon sign is flashing '24-hour +'. It looks like the symbol for a round-the-clock chemist: but no, it's to alert those in the area to a different kind of first aid. A few doors along is San Anton, a Catholic church that provides a 24/7 service to the homeless and others who find themselves in need of friendship, food and shelter.

It's 9pm when I arrive, and sure enough the church doors are wide open, and the light and warmth and bustle of people is spilling out onto the street.

San Anton, it's clear, is the vibrant hub of the neighbourhood, a place where casual passers-by are welcomed along with regular visitors. Inside, the space combines a traditional Latino church with the sights and sounds of the Church's social teaching in action. Instead of pews, the back few rows of seating are benches with narrow trestle

> Madrid, in the throes of an ongoing financial crisis, has plenty of people who sleep rough; to him, it made no sense to close a space where they could find warmth, and shelter, and safety

tables, onto which bowls and spoons are being put out. 'They're laying the tables for breakfast – people who are homeless can eat here, we have up to 200 people a day,' explains Lucia Lopez, who works in the church's administrative offices. Further up the church, the benches are covered with soft pads so that people who have nowhere else to go can sleep in reasonable comfort. On the wall is a sign advertising some of the services available in the church: drinking water, toilets with baby changing facilities, phone charging, and wifi. In another corner the traditional confessionals have been boarded up, and instead there's a coffee table and two comfortable armchairs where the parish priest, Fr Angel Garcia, and his fellow priests are happy to hear confessions. There are several Masses daily, and throughout the evening the sound of gentle plainchant is piped through the church lest anyone should forget, amidst the hurly-burly, that this is a house of God.

Halfway up the church, a red curtain screens off the altar and the first few rows of seats, so that those who want to pray quietly may do so. The central altar is a conventional one with a tabernacle and statues: but on either side are large banners with quotes from Pope Francis about the importance of caring for the poor, and of how vital is it that churches keep their doors open.

He may have meant it figuratively, but when Fr Angel took over the parish – his first ever parish, at the age of almost 80 – he chose to take it literally. Madrid, in the throes of an ongoing financial crisis, has plenty of people who sleep rough; to him, it made no sense to close a space where they could find warmth, and shelter, and safety. The Archbishop of Madrid backed his plan to keep the church open 24/7, and a team of volunteers was recruited to run it. Not everyone likes the idea; but Fr Angel has never held back from putting his interpretation of the Gospel values into practice. More than 50 years ago, as a young priest in his mid-twenties only recently ordained, he set up the Messengers of Peace, a charity devoted to alleviating distress both in his native Spain and in the wider world. Today the Messengers of Peace is a world-class NGO with 50,000 staff and volunteers working in countries across the world, including in front-line communities in Syria and war-torn African countries.

Fr Angel, who like many Spanish priests wears a tie rather than a clerical collar, radiates warmth, laughter and fun: almost every question I ask him meets with a smile and a jolly answer. What made him set up the Messengers of Peace all those years ago? 'I was young, and I was crazy,' he says. But seriously? 'I grew up in the aftermath of the Spanish civil war, in the north of Spain. I was from a generation that knew hunger and sadness. There were many widows, and there had been much bloodshed. There were many needs to meet, and I was inspired by St John Bosco and by the parish priest of my village to help meet those needs.' In Franco-run Spain, he was often regarded as leftwing and revolutionary. 'But there was a church leader at the time called Cardinal Tarancon who was an important figure at Vatican II, and he always supported me.'

> **His hard work and commitment paid off, and amongst other honours he's been nominated for the Nobel Peace Prize**

He never imagined back then how much his charity would grow. 'I never had time for dreams or plans – it just grew slowly, through the years,' he says.

But his hard work and commitment paid off, and amongst other honours he's been nominated for the Nobel Peace Prize. If he ever received, he says, he'd share it with the thousands who have worked alongside him for the Messengers of Peace. 'I believe in people, in the goodness of people,' he says. 'I've been loved and supported by so many people – you can never do work like this alone.'

> As well as his remarkable church, he runs a restaurant half a mile up the road; and it's a restaurant with a difference

While we've been talking, a teenage boy called Josua has been standing patiently beside us, listening to the conversation. And here's another surprise about this mould-breaking priest: Josua is his son.

Fr Angel adopted him as a baby from El Salvador; the boy had been horribly injured in a fire in his home, and by taking him on, Fr Angel enabled him to have the medical treatment he needed in Spain.

So how has it been parenting Josua alongside his church work? Well, he says, Josua does have a mum; but he's been very involved in his life, and Josua calls him 'Papa'. 'The truth is, being a parent is the most important thing in my life, as it is for any parent,' he says. 'Josua was the best present I could ever have; he changed my life.'

And Fr Angel, in turn, is changing other lives. As well as his remarkable church, he runs a restaurant half a mile up the road; and it's a restaurant with a difference. By day the Robin Hood cafe, as it's called, is pretty much your average Madrid eaterie: there's a blackboard offering a three-course menu at 15 Euros, and cured hams sit on the counter at the front. It's a popular place for lunch for both workers in the area, and passing tourists. By night it looks much the same, with similar food on offer – but at this point the meals are free, to homeless people and others who have nowhere else to eat; the money taken from the paying customers is used to finance the meals for the poor. The restaurant's name is its mission – although, says Fr Angel, the idea isn't so much to rob from the rich to help the poor, as to enable those who are wealthier to share what they have with those less fortunate.

Like San Anton, the Robin Hood is a hive of activity on the evening of my visit: there are two sittings for supper, with 50 meals served at each. Men and women, old and young, are sitting at tables set for four, chatting and laughing. 'One of the things this restaurant means is that homeless people can enjoy eating,' says Fr Angel. 'They can eat in a convivial and friendly atmosphere, they're not rushed, and they're treated exactly as the paying guests are during the day.'

 Pope Francis is a blessing for us; it's meant the Catholic Church is the way I always dreamed it could be

On the wall is a sign that sums up the philosophy of Fr Angel and the Robin Hood. 'Menu del Dia', it announces: first course friendship; second course dignity; third course companionship. It is, says the redoubtable priest, a simple formula; his life's work has been based on the straightforward desire to treat those in need as equals, and to share so that everyone has enough. Both at San Anton and at the Robin Hood, it's not easy to tell who are the volunteers and who are the homeless: both church and restaurant are melting-pots, reminders that there isn't much difference between people, and that we have more in common as human beings than we have divisions because of economic circumstance.

Unsurprisingly, Fr Angel is a big fan of Pope Francis, who he has been to Rome to meet. 'Pope Francis is a blessing for us; it's meant the Catholic Church is the way I always dreamed it could be,' says Fr Angel with a grateful smile. 'For me, the church has always been about far more than the cardinals and the bishops and the priests. It's about the people, and that's the vision I hope we're putting into action here in Madrid.'

10

The nun they call Atilla

Sister Rita Lee is a champion for the beleaguered residents of an impoverished inner-city area.

'I have come that all may have life, and have it to the full.' These words from St John's Gospel are the first thing you see when you arrive at the Lalley Centre in Manchester; and they sum up its *raison d'être*, and that of the dynamic nun at its centre, Sister Rita Lee – who's also known, round these parts, as 'Attila the Nun'.

Sister Rita is 71 years old, stocky, with glasses and wearing the kind of blue suit that screams 'nun out of habit' to any veteran Catholic. The Lalley Centre is her domain: she founded it ten years ago, and she is its pivotal figure. It's a drop-in centre for those in need, and given its location, slap bang in the middle of perhaps Manchester's poorest neighbourhood, Collyhurst, that means the people who come here really are in need. 'Most of them aren't working, they haven't been able to find a job,'

> What I don't do is judge them, because we don't know all the details and we tend to make up our minds about people too quickly

says Sister Rita, who's a trained social worker. 'And some of them don't have enough money for food and heating: they're having to make a choice, eat or heat. The ones with children sometimes haven't got the money to buy clothes or shoes for them; sometimes they're having problems getting them into school, or difficulties with their benefits.'

No-one can wave a magic wand for people whose lives are in such deep difficulties, but Sister Rita comes pretty close. 'What I believe in,' she says, 'are instant solutions. I don't like this approach where people have to go and catch two or three buses to get to this office and that office for the help they need, or when they're told to come back next week. Their lives are hard enough already; we've got to do better for them than that. What I do is get everything sorted, right here and right now.'

In action she's reminiscent of a female equivalent of the Godfather; a Godmother, perhaps. Visitors to the centre are invited, according to a sign on the wall of the sunny cafeteria, to have two free cups of tea or coffee, and two free slices of toast (extra items 10p each), while they wait for the chance to see her. They are ushered into her presence in an office with a sign saying 'St Jude' on the door: he's the patron saint of hopeless cases, but no-one is beyond hope for Sister Rita. Visitors sit down on the sofa in her office, and she listens to their story. 'What I don't do is judge them, because we don't know all the details and we tend to make up our minds about people too quickly,' she says.

Among the 69 people who came to the centre this morning ('that's about average,' says Sister Rita) was a mother of three who desperately needs new beds for her children, and another woman ('who was in a real state, very upset') whose son owed thousands of pounds. 'The people who need their money back are coming to her house and banging on her door – and it's not her fault, and it's certainly not the fault of her other children, but they're all suffering,' she says. The woman doesn't want to go to the Lalley food bank, which is a few minutes' walk from the centre, and Sister Rita understands that. 'So what we're going to do for that woman,' she says, 'is make up a food parcel and give it to her here, so she doesn't need to go to the food bank. For the woman who needs beds, she's already called the local SVP centre to ask if they have some in their depot – they do, so that problem will soon be solved.'

A few months ago, Sister Rita's can-do attitude netted her a real coup. 'I was lying in bed one night, thinking how can we help these people, and we're seeing more and more of them, who fall foul of the benefits sanctions,' she remembers. Sanctions are often handed out without regard, she believes, to what's actually going on in a benefit claimant's life. 'And then I thought, I've got it,' she says. 'I'll write to that fella who's in charge of it, and to the Prime Minister, and I'll ask them to fix it.' The fella in question was Iain Duncan Smith, Secretary of State for Work and Pensions (she was unaware, at the time, that he was a fellow Catholic). She was invited to a meeting with him ('I think, to be honest, that he was a bit in awe of me... that's what it felt like anyway') and lo and behold, a team of officers from the Department for Work and Pensions now

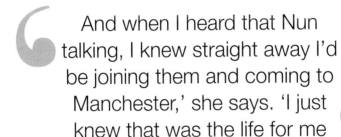

And when I heard that Nun talking, I knew straight away I'd be joining them and coming to Manchester,' she says. 'I just knew that was the life for me

come to the Lalley Centre weekly to talk to people who have had sanctions against them, and to restore their benefits if they didn't deserve them.

On the wall of the Lalley Centre reception there's a picture from the 1940s of a group of white-clad first communicants with the priest. It harks back to a time when the Church in Britain was a different world, a kind of protective world for its community. In many ways, the Lalley Centre is a throwback to that era; and there's nothing wrong with that, certainly for the residents of Collyhurst. What's more, the protection the Church once afforded its own community certainly isn't restricted to Catholics in Sister Rita's 21st century version. 'I don't care who comes in here – I want to help them all,' she says. 'I don't care about the colour of their skin, I don't care what country they came from, I don't care which religion they practise.

They're all equally welcome here; giving a welcome is one of the things we do, one of the things we ought to do, one of the things that makes a difference

They're all equally welcome here; giving a welcome is one of the things we do, one of the things we ought to do, one of the things that makes a difference.' Added to which, she says, 'in my head there's one God. We might call him different names, and worship him in different ways, but he's the same God. I thank Almighty God every day that

I'm a Christian and a Catholic, but that's because it's what works for me. I couldn't do the work I do, day in and day out, without knowing God is right beside me, working with me. I ask for his help, and the things that need to be done always are done.'

Sister Rita attributes her success as a 'fixer' for Collyhurst down to various things: the fact that she herself was raised in poverty in Ireland, her sense of humour, and what she calls having a heart for the poor. 'You couldn't do this work if you didn't have a heart for the poor,' she says. 'Sympathy isn't enough; you have to have empathy as well. I knew poverty in my youth, and I thank God for it.' All the same, she's certainly no soft touch: hard-luck stories are checked up on, and woe betide anyone who comes to her with lies about their needs. 'I don't put up with any nonsense,' she says. 'If there's any trouble I go and shout at people.'

She's been a Presentation Sister since she was 17; like so much else in her life, it was all instant with Sister Rita. She found school difficult, partly because she was deaf but her deafness wasn't recognised or allowances made for it; so when a Presentation nun came in to talk about vocations, she was put at the front so she couldn't misbehave. 'And when I heard that nun talking, I knew straight away I'd be joining them and coming to Manchester,' she says. 'I just knew that was the life for me.'

> The problem with Collyhurst – which is only minutes from the sparkling high-rise centre of Manchester – is that it has no supermarket, no hairdresser, no newsagent's and no café. But people need these places to create a community

Today the residents of Collyhurst thank their God, whichever God they worship, that she did. And having alleviated the difficulties in so many individual lives in the ten years since she set up the Lalley Centre, she's now got her sights set on an even bigger prize – local regeneration. The problem with Collyhurst – which is only minutes from the sparkling high-rise centre of Manchester – is that it has no supermarket, no hairdresser, no newsagent's and no café. 'But people need these places to create a community,' she says; and her next big plan is to talk to the city council about what can be done to create more infrastructure. It's hard to imagine Sister Rita is going to fail; with her behind it, Collyhurst is undoubtedly on the up.

11

The Anglican priest who's a high-profile role model for women of colour

Rev Rose Hudson-Wilkin is chaplain to the Houses of Parliament, frequently to be seen on TV on State occasions.

Most of the black women who work in Parliament are cleaners or caterers, and if Rose Hudson-Wilkin didn't wear a dog collar, she would probably be mistaken for one of them. Not that there's anything wrong with being a cleaner or caterer, as she's quick to point out. But she's a priest, the chaplain to the Houses of Parliament, and a staunch campaigner for greater visibility for people of colour in high-ranking positions.

Rose grew up in Jamaica: as she puts it, she had the great good fortune to grow up there, because it meant she was surrounded by black women and men who fulfilled all roles in society, including the highest of posts. 'Everywhere I looked, there were people just like me,' she says. 'So I knew I could do anything I wanted with my life. It's so powerful to be able to see your reflection in others.'

> We were fortunate, because there was a shortage of priests at the time and that meant the people shared the task of leading the worship

Her early life in Jamaica was no picnic, though. When Rose was just a year old, her mother went to live in the UK. Probably, she says, the plan was to send for her and her sister, who remained in Montego Bay with their father: but somehow the summons never came, both her parents found new partners, and it wasn't until she was nine that she met her mother again, when her mother returned to Jamaica.

The lack of a mother didn't mean a lack of love, but it was the kind of love that's shown in actions, and cuddles and endearments were in short supply. Much of her validation came from the extended community at her church: the other worshippers were always there for her, Rose recalls, interested in her school career and her life and plans. 'We were fortunate, because there was a shortage of priests at the time and that meant the people shared the task of leading the worship. So sometimes it was the turn of the young people to lead, and that gave me amazing experiences. I preached my first sermon at 14!'

Around the same time, she began to wonder whether God was calling her to the priesthood. 'One night I had a dream that disturbed me, and I couldn't go back to sleep,' she remembers. 'I reached for my Bible, and it fell open at Luke 4 – 'The spirit of the Lord is upon me' – and I thought, wow. And the next day the reading was from the same passage in Isaiah. I thought, this is no coincidence – it's a call.'

The only problem was that women were not at that time being ordained in the Anglican church: but Rose was unperturbed. 'I thought, I'll just trust in God. I believe I'm being called, and I'll obey that call. If God wants me, things will change.' She joined the Church Army, and was sent to the UK for training, and while there met her husband Ken, a Geordie who was later ordained. The couple had three children (now adults and there are also four grandchildren), and for the next few years Rose focused on being a mother – but she never forgot her calling, or her belief that her time would come. As her children got older, and after the Anglican church admitted women to the diaconate, she applied for the training course, was ordained in 1991, and became one of the cohort of women deacons who were waiting eagerly when the Church of England ordained women for the first time in 1994.

Parishes followed, first as a curate and later as a parish priest – and there were difficulties sometimes with churchgoers who were not comfortable with the idea of women's ordination. Being a black woman priest made her an outsider twice over, she says: but she was determined to see the positive changes, and the fact that this was the moment to claim her inheritance – not just on her own behalf, but on behalf of young black people and women everywhere, who could now see the church hierarchy as belonging to them, as being open to all. The Archbishop of York, John Sentamu, was a strong ally, and she spent more than 10 years building up strong and vibrant parishes in east London.

More than a decade seemed long enough in her job, and she was starting to think about moving on when Ken phoned her one day with some news. She was in Jamaica at the time: Ken was calling to

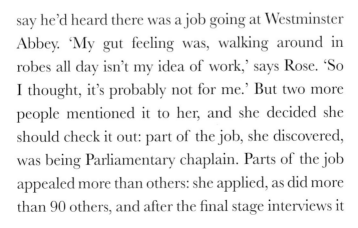

Being a black woman priest made her an outsider twice over, she says: but she was determined to see the positive changes, and the fact that this was the moment to claim her inheritance

say he'd heard there was a job going at Westminster Abbey. 'My gut feeling was, walking around in robes all day isn't my idea of work,' says Rose. 'So I thought, it's probably not for me.' But two more people mentioned it to her, and she decided she should check it out: part of the job, she discovered, was being Parliamentary chaplain. Parts of the job appealed more than others: she applied, as did more than 90 others, and after the final stage interviews it was decided to change the way the role is organised, so Rose remained in her parish but take on the role of Parliamentary chaplain as well.

We meet in her office in the Palace of Westminster: it's off the hallway of the Speaker's House, and while we're chatting John Bercow appears with his children, back from the school run, and the two greet

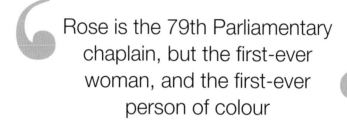

Rose is the 79th Parliamentary chaplain, but the first-ever woman, and the first-ever person of colour

one another warmly. Rose's role at Westminster is closely connected with Bercow's: each day at the start of the sitting in the House of Commons, she delivers the prayers for the day. 'MPs often come up to me afterwards and say how moving they find the prayers, and how important they are to everything that happens there,' she says. She doesn't say prayers in the House of Lords because the bishops who sit there lead on that; but she also leads two communion services a week in the beautiful chapel of the Palace of Westminster, as well as officiating at weddings and baptisms (staff and members of the Houses are entitled to use the chapel for their family occasions).

Rose is the 79th Parliamentary chaplain, but the first-ever woman, and the first-ever person of colour. As at other moments in her life, she's a trailblazer. 'I feel like Esther,' she says, 'who was told: you are here for such a time as this. I am able to be visible here, and I go off around Britain giving talks and preaching. I especially enjoy giving talks in schools, because I'm so aware of how important it is that the young people of today see someone like me in a job like this.'

She's long been spoken of as a likely bishop; she's not ruling it out but nor is she holding out for it either. 'I'm not holding my breath,' she says, 'but if I'm called to serve then it would be something I'd consider. The important thing is to be focused on what you're doing, and I'm still very much focused on life at Westminster.'

When I ask what's been the highpoint of her seven years at Westminster, she answers without missing a beat: that's an easy one. 'Without a shadow of a doubt, it was meeting Barack Obama. I was wearing a floral coat dress and he took my hand and he said: "man, you look spiff".' And she throws

> She throws back her head and laughs, a big, happy laugh, remembering that moment when the most powerful leader on earth met the chaplain of the Palace of Westminster, and both revelled for a few moments in their shared african roots

back her head and laughs, a big, happy laugh, remembering that moment when the most powerful leader on earth met the chaplain of the Palace of Westminster, and both revelled for a few moments in their shared African roots, how far they'd come, and how important it was that they'd made their respective journeys.

12

The single mother who lost her only child – but is determined to go on finding life 'amazing', because that's what her daughter did

Anne-Marie Cockburn's daughter Martha was 15 when she died after taking what she thought was 'safe' ecstasy.

Anne-Marie Cockburn wrote the following words on 21 July 2013: 'My 15-year-old daughter died yesterday. I watched them try to save her. They pumped her chest and drilled something into her leg, but I knew she was already dead on arrival at the hospital. They elevated her arms, but I don't know why: her eyes were half-open and she was way beyond the clouds and stars already.'

The previous morning, a sunny Saturday, Anne-Marie was the happy mother of a healthy child. She and Martha were close, perhaps in a way only a single mother and her only daughter can be. It was just the two of them in their cosy flat in Oxford and they did everything together. Earlier that week they had been to Ikea to buy new stuff for Martha's bedroom; the following weekend, they were off to Bristol. That day, Martha went kayaking with friends on a lake across town and Anne-Marie went shopping.

 Today she thinks of herself as a 'non-practising' Mother; because she'll always be a mother, the woman who bore Martha

But by Sunday morning, Martha was dead: Anne-Marie woke up to an entirely changed identity. 'There's no word for what I'd become – maybe it's too terrible a situation to have a word for,' she says. 'I'm not a widow or an orphan or a divorcee – they all have a word.

'To describe what I am, I need nine words: "I'm a single mother whose only child is dead".' Today she thinks of herself as a 'non-practising' mother; because she'll always be a mother, the woman who bore Martha. She's made up a word to describe herself, too: smothered. 'That's "s" for "single", and then "mother", and "ed" is for "expired daughter",' she explains.

Smothered could also describe the effect of losing her child. It could explain the impact of the magnitude of grief on this slight, 42-year-old woman who says she never really looked for another partner after finding herself alone with a 10-month-old baby because Martha was enough.

Yet the last thing grief has done to Anne-Marie is smother her. In many ways, she says, she feels more alive than ever. It's as though her antennae are twice as sensitive and she's seeing the world in extra-sharp focus because of what she's been through.

She notices every detail, is attuned to every nuance that underlines the gulf between the way she was, and the way she is now. 'The other day I looked down at a bag with someone's shopping, and I saw a box that said family tissues,' she says. 'I thought, I don't need those any more, I can just buy packets for one.'

Another time she and a friend went on a train journey that they'd usually have made with Martha. 'I was about to get out my family railcard and then I stopped and said, I can't use this any more, can I? And they said, you need a child to travel with you to use that. And I thought, I don't have a child to travel with any more.'

This is red-raw, unadulterated, up-close grief: and what's remarkable about Anne-Marie is that she's chosen to share the immediate grief of the early hours, days, weeks and months – and of now – with the rest of us.

Writing has been her therapy since the day Martha died. 'Writing it down felt right,' she says. 'I've always written a diary and when I started writing this down, it poured out. On the second day my parents physically took the notebook and pen out of my hands and said, you've got to have a shower. I was just writing, writing.'

Now, when she reads what she wrote in those first few days, it's as if she's finding out what she was doing for the first time. 'You forget everything in the shock of early grief. Writing it down straight away

> You forget everything in the shock of early grief. Writing it down straight away is the only way of remembering what happened and I need to remember it because I need to make sense of it

is the only way of remembering what happened and I need to remember it because I need to make sense of it,' she says.

She published her diary, she explains, because of the way Martha died. What happened on that July day by the lake in Oxford was that Martha took what she thought was MDMA, better known as ecstasy. Shortly before 12.45pm, Anne-Marie texted her daughter to tell her the name of the hotel she'd booked in Bristol for the following weekend. Martha responded simply: 'Cute.'

'That meant she approved,' smiles Anne-Marie. 'She was looking forward to going away.'

Half an hour later, a number she didn't recognise flashed up on Anne-Marie's phone. She answered and the world as she'd known it for 15 years ended. 'It was a woman calling. She said: "Your daughter

> All that makes sense to Anne-Marie is to document the experience in the hope that others will learn from it

is gravely ill and we are trying to save her,"' Anne-Marie remembers. A friend drove her to hospital, but Martha hadn't arrived. 'They told me they had no notification of the incident, and it was only when I said that the woman in the park had told me they'd called the air ambulance that they realised how serious it was and showed me to a side-room.' When the ambulance arrived (Martha was brought by road in the end, because she wasn't stable enough to travel by air), Anne-Marie was ushered into the emergency room where the crash team was desperately working on her. 'But I knew, the second

I saw her, that she was dead,' says Anne-Marie. In her book, she describes what happened next. 'I was calling to her in the tone I last heard when I gave birth to her.' And then: 'I couldn't breathe once they announced what I already knew: my fingers and toes were tingling. They put me on a wheeled chair and asked me what I wanted to do. What do I want to do? I don't know what to do – what do you do in a situation like this?'

In many ways that question has become a daily mantra in Anne-Marie's mind. Just as there is no name for her condition, so there is no blueprint, no strategy, no recipe for dealing with a loss like hers. There are no children to carry on for and there's no partner to keep her going.

All that makes sense to Anne-Marie is to document the experience in the hope that others will learn from it. She knows that happened among Martha's friends in Oxford. 'Some said they'd never touch drugs – they didn't realise how dangerous something like Ecstasy could be.'

She hopes parents of teenagers will ask more questions, take the threat of drugs more seriously.

'Because it wasn't just Martha – so many teenagers are buying and taking drugs. I honestly believe that if it could happen to us, it could happen to anyone. She couldn't have imagined that this could mean the end of her life, at the age of 15.' Anne-Marie now campaigns for the legalisation and regulation of recreational drugs, which she believes would have prevented Martha's death and would prevent the loss of other young people in the future: if they were able to buy clearly labelled drugs from regulated sources, she argues, they would know it was safe. The drug Martha was sold was 91% pure compared with an average street level of 58%; the teenager had assumed that the better quality, the safer it would be. Tragically she didn't realise that the exact opposite was the case, and that the batch she was sold was so concentrated that it was deadly.

A few months after Martha's death, on what would have been her 16th birthday, a group of her friends joined Anne-Marie in the park where she died, and at 6.41am, the exact time she was born, they lit lanterns by the lake in her memory. Anne-Marie felt a responsibility to be there for Martha's many friends, for whom her death could hardly have been more shocking. 'So many of them have been deeply affected by it – I want to help them find peace and to remember her.'

Remembering Martha is never difficult for her mother. 'If I just close my eyes I can still feel the brush of her lips against my cheek,' she says. The

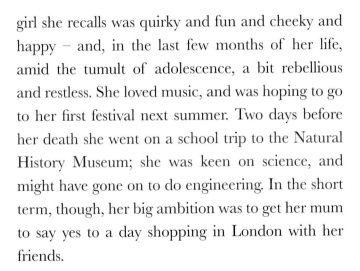

> The girl she recalls was quirky and fun and cheeky and happy

girl she recalls was quirky and fun and cheeky and happy – and, in the last few months of her life, amid the tumult of adolescence, a bit rebellious and restless. She loved music, and was hoping to go to her first festival next summer. Two days before her death she went on a school trip to the Natural History Museum; she was keen on science, and might have gone on to do engineering. In the short term, though, her big ambition was to get her mum to say yes to a day shopping in London with her friends.

Anne-Marie has memories, too, of travelling the world with Martha. 'I'm so grateful that we saw so many places, went on so many trips,' she says. 'When

I was 15 I'd only been to Germany: but Martha had been to America and Croatia, France and Greece, Ireland and Italy, Spain and Singapore. She rode on a camel in Egypt, went on an elephant in Bali, snorkelled on the Great Barrier Reef. She lived for 5,742 days, seven hours and 36 minutes, and her life was full of adventure – and I'm so happy I shared so many of those adventures with her.'

 Martha thought life was amazing. And I still think life is amazing

How does Anne-Marie live her life, now that her daughter is gone? 'I could have become a crazy cat lady,' she says. 'I could have had a breakdown. I could have just given up and never gone out again. 'But Martha thought life was amazing. And I still think life is amazing. I wish it could be amazing with her still in it, but it can't. It can only be amazing without her. And I'm doing my best to make it that.'

Martha

13

The child torn away from her family who went on to help a million children on the other side of the world

Christina Noble was only ten when she was taken to an institution: but out of her misery grew a charity that has transformed the lives of street children.

Christina Noble's upbringing in the Dublin slums in the 1940s was so bad that it barely merits the name 'childhood' at all. Life delivered a series of unbelievably devastating blows that came along in such quick succession that it is hard to believe she ever managed to get up again. But not only did she get up: she went on to found a charity that has helped nigh-on a million children across Asia, and counting.

Noble's story is powerful, and it's the subject of an eponymous movie directed by Stephen Bradley and starring Deirdre O'Kane in the lead role and Brendan Coyle of Downton Abbey. The film traces her early days as a child in an area of Dublin called The Liberties – 'it was the worst slum in Europe,' she tells me – after she was born there in 1944, the eldest girl in a family of eight children, two of whom

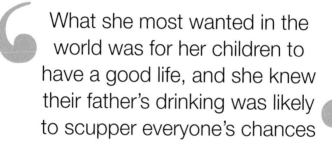

What she most wanted in the world was for her children to have a good life, and she knew their father's drinking was likely to scupper everyone's chances

died as babies. They were desperately poor, and had to survive in a one-bedroom flat, with the living room serving as the room where the children slept; the bedroom, where her parents spent their nights on a mattress on the floor, also functioned as dining room and sitting room.

Despite being poor, says Noble, the family just about managed to stay on track in the early days; her mother, Annie, was a kind and gentle woman who prayed a lot, belonged to the Legion of Mary, and used to busy herself, in the slivers of free time she must only occasionally have had, with visiting those who were even sicker, and poorer, than she herself was. Annie was never healthy; she had a bad heart, and then TB. And she had another cross to bear: an alcoholic husband. Like so many Irish women of her time, she never touched drink herself; but there was a sadness about her, says Noble, because what she most wanted in the world was for her children to have a good life, and she knew their father's drinking was likely to scupper everyone's chances. Noble remembers, as a young child, being sent to look for him in the pubs. 'He'd start drinking and he'd drink and drink and drink,' she says. 'I'd go from pub to pub looking for him, and when I eventually found him I'd say "come home Daddy" – even though there was nothing to eat in the house at all.'

Noble was ten when her mother died: she remembers making a pact with God that, if he let her live, she'd become a Carmelite and devote the rest of her life to prayer. But her mother did die; and instead of becoming a nun, Noble became a mother to her younger siblings – they even called her 'Mammy'. She was a child of ten, caring for a boy of seven, and two girls of five and two, her brother Johnny and her sisters Kathy and Philomena. 'I didn't know how to look after children,' she says sadly. Some days all they had to eat were a few biscuits to dip into their tea; other days, there was nothing at all.

They were at least together; but all that was about to change. When Noble had to take her younger siblings, who were now painfully thin, and had scabies and ringworm, to hospital, they were reported to the authorities. 'A few days later a man in a peaked cap came to see us; I remember him knocking on the door and asking where we slept,' she says. 'They came back the following morning and took us away.'

The children were taken, not to a friendly foster mother, but to a cold courtroom. Their father was there too, and a judge. Noble remembers not being sure what was about to happen, and then realising in a flash, just before it actually happened. 'The judge said we were to be removed from our father,' she says. That was bad enough; but there was worse. 'And then he said that, as I was a bad influence on them, I had to go to a separate institution.' She was, she admits, a sassy and spirited child – her big talent was singing, and her mother had dreamed with her that she would go on to be a second Doris Day – but she certainly wasn't the wicked influence the judge was inferring. Her account of the children being forcibly separated from their father – him repeating the mantra 'it's for the best', her pleading with him

> There was plenty more misery ahead: for some reason all the children were told that their siblings were dead,so it was many years before they were reunited

not to let it happen, still believing in that way kids do believe, that their parents can overcome any obstacle – is hard to listen to, and hard to watch in the movie. But away they were taken, in a big Black Maria; and first her brother was dropped at an institution, and then Noble at hers; she remembers the faces of her little sisters as they were driven away from her.

There was plenty more misery ahead: for some reason all the children were told that their siblings were dead, so it was many years before they were reunited. Noble escaped from one institution, and was for a while billeted with distant relatives, but was sexually abused; she ended up as a street child, before having a baby at 16 and then entering into a marriage that proved abusive. It was suffering

She went to Vietnam in 1989, stepped off her plane, and immediately connected with the street children who were everywhere in Ho Chi Minh City

heaped on suffering; and then one day, in the midst of her tribulations, she had a dream in which she felt called to travel to Vietnam to care for street children. 'You might laugh,' she says. 'You might say only an Irish eejit would act on a dream as if it was a message from God. And maybe you'd be right. But I did it; I went and did it, and I'll never be able to quite explain why or how.'

She went to Vietnam in 1989, stepped off her plane, and immediately connected with the street children who were everywhere in Ho Chi Minh City. 'They were just like me and my silblings,' she says. 'They had nothing, and they had no-one looking out for them.' And so Noble became their champion; and a pretty unorthodox champion at that. In the movie she is seen smuggling a couple of little girls into her room so she can give them a bath and some food, before taking them out to buy clothes. And this direct approach has become her trademark: today the Christina Noble foundation sponsors children across Vietnam and Mongolia, and helps provide education and healthcare for many hundreds of thousands.

Noble divides her time between Brighton and Vietnam. Like many Irish children of her generation, there were times when she knew suffering at the hands of priests and nuns, and even in Vietnam there have been times when the Church has been less than helpful – on one occasion, she asked a Mercedes-driving priest to help fund a children's medical centre. When he seemed keen, said he'd talk to his parishioners, and then sent a parcel that felt like a stack of money, she was thrilled. She thanked God before she opened the packet; inside were hundreds of prayer cards, and a note from the priest on which he'd written: 'You are doing wonderful work…God bless you. We will pray for you.' It took her back to Ireland, she says, to 'the times when I had gone to the church for help. They gave me prayers to wear on my feet and prayers to eat.'

> I'm a bit of a fruit cake, but I believe the good is in what you do in your life

What's most impressive about Noble is what she's achieved for the children of Vietnam; but what's also impressive is that she's still a Catholic, still a believer, still a Mass-goer. In the movie she is seen, time after time, going to church to light a candle; when things go against her, instead of thinking God has given up on her, she goes to have a stern word with him. 'Of course I still pray,' she tells me. 'I'm a bit of a fruit cake, but I believe the good is in what you do in your life. Nothing I went through ever put me off God, though it did sometimes put me off the Church. But there are good nuns and priest out there – life is about individuals, and there are many good nuns and good priests in the world.'

Christina with children in Vietnam

14

Guy Stagg had been battling depression when he decided to go on pilgrimage - and kept on going

In the summer of 2012, on a whim and with no experience of long-distance walking, Guy Stagg decided to trek the 60 or so miles from his home in London to Canterbury. Three years out of university, where he had battled against depression and alcoholism, he'd recently sought medical help to overcome his problems, and wondered whether walking might be beneficial.

Canterbury appealed to him, for its role 'at the beginning of English literature' – he had been an English student at Cambridge. He set off having done virtually no planning, and arrived in Chaucer's city two days later. He had walked under baking sun and driving rain with little protection, his heels bruised and his socks clotted with the blood from burst blisters.

 Having endured months when he was too afraid to even leave his room, walking had broadened his vista – 'making the world wide again'

But as he lay on the grass outside the cathedral, it wasn't pain that registered – it was relief, 'the deep calm that lies on the other side of tiredness'. Having endured months when he was too afraid to even leave his room, walking had broadened his vista – 'making the world wide again', he writes in his book, *The Crossway*, about the role walking played in his recovery from depression.

Looking around, he noticed a stone on which was written the name of an ancient pilgrim route, the Via Francigena. And in that moment, Guy made an extraordinary decision: to keep right on walking, following the path carved out by medieval Christians on the way to the tombs of Saints Peter and Paul in Rome. A few days later, having researched the journey some more, he became bolder still: now he'd press on to an even further holy city, Jerusalem, 5,500 km away. He wasn't exactly sure why, he tells me when we meet at a central London café on a sunny morning, but of one thing he was certain: walking offered him something he needed: some healing, some respite and ultimately some hope.

'I didn't understand why I was going, and I didn't want to interrogate it too fully,' he explains. 'I was being reckless, naive – and while I wasn't entirely sure why, I believed it would help me to do this walk. I knew if I thought too much about it, I'd come up with reasons not to go. So I organised things as quickly as I could, and set out on 1 January 2013.' He did more planning than he had for the Canterbury walk – but not a lot. Unlike the Camino to Santiago de Compostela, a route that thousands of people follow each year, the Via Francigena isn't very popular or commercialised, and there's nothing like the huge amount of information available on it in books or online.

Leaving in the winter made little sense – 'It was

cold, and the days were short and dark. I got lost many times' – and he hadn't even arranged where he was going to stay. 'The hotels were too expensive: but what I realised was that if you went to a church or mosque along the route and explained what you were doing, they would help. I was like a medieval pilgrim: I had no plan, I simply trusted I'd find shelter.'

Guy had grown up in a church-going family and knew about some of the rituals of faith; but as he walked, he says, his insights on the role they play in human life changed.

'I grew up, as many do, with the understanding that religion is a bunch of arguments about how the world works, and either you accept them or you reject them. But I've come to realise that's not the whole story. Religion is about a lot more than belief: it's about being in touch with something that's moving and meaningful.'

Many elements of religious worship, he realised, are good for our mental health. 'If you go down on your knees, you're humbling yourself, and that punctures the sense of yourself as the centre of the universe. On a pilgrimage you journey into the unknown and you have to ask others for help. So these are helpful experiences: they make you more grateful, less self-absorbed. They're good for your mental health.'

 These are helpful experiences: they make you more grateful, less self-absorbed. They're good for your mental health

Guy met many interesting people and visited endless fascinating places along his journey – although there were frightening moments as well. In the Alps, he was stuck in a snowstorm and was smuggled into a monastery by a kind monk who took pity on him. In Lebanon, he got caught up in a terrorist attack. He describes the peace of dawn prayer at an Orthodox monastery on Mount Athos, the kindness of the Frenchwoman who bought him ice soles when she heard he was planning to cross the snowy mountains on foot, and the Turkish mosques where he was given dolma, goat's cheese, olives, and endless cups of tea.

But around the mid-point of the journey, he hit despair. Having had high hopes for the benefits of the walk, he felt it wasn't working. 'I was still full of my memories, and my symptoms were returning. In Rome I had a panic attack, and I started drinking again. I thought, this journey is having the opposite

> I realised I would have to go through the experiences I'd been trying to ignore; I had to face my demons, move through the pain

effect to what I hoped.' Now, he says, he can see that hitting rock bottom was a necessary part of the journey back to health. 'I realised I would have to go through the experiences I'd been trying to ignore; I had to face my demons, move through the pain.'

Unlike his arrival in Canterbury, getting to Jerusalem after almost 10 months turned out to be an anticlimax. 'I felt very confused,' he remembers. 'There was no big sense of triumph, no sudden epiphany.' He stayed in the area for a few days, musing that the point of pilgrimage is much more about the travelling than it is about the destination. 'It made me realise that the destinations we set ourselves are arbitrary: they're the excuse to do the journey, but what matters are the day-to-day experiences: they're what give a pilgrimage value. They're the purpose of it all.'

And the value of pilgrimage, it turned out, wasn't completed when the end-point was reached. Instead, he has continued to ponder it and, little by little, begun to understand how it has helped him recover. 'When I got to the end I knew something important had happened, but I wasn't sure what it was. It was through writing the book that I was able to digest the experience. The main things I took from it were the kindness of strangers, which gave me new hope in humankind, and a newfound sense of purpose and meaning in my life, which I realised through writing, and the knowledge that I had this story I wanted to share.'

He is, he says, in 'a completely different place now. I'm not sure where my mental illness came from – it started during my time at university, and there was no original trauma or life event that explained it.' The low point was after he graduated: most people, he says, 'leave university feeling their life is about to begin; I felt mine was ending'. And it almost did end: at one point, he made a serious suicide attempt, though failed to disclose the reason for his injuries when he was taken to hospital. During the time he was mentally ill, he says, he felt controlled by his

> When I was ill I'd get a thought in my mind and be unable to get rid of it. These days I can experience negative emotions, but they don't knock me off course the way they did in the past

thoughts. Today, that's turned around. 'One of the ways of thinking about mental illness is that you lose the ability to choose what you think about,' he says. 'When I was ill I'd get a thought in my mind and be unable to get rid of it. These days I can experience negative emotions, but they don't knock me off course the way they did in the past.'

Now 30, he's working on another book, and the world seems to hold promise again. And if the practices of faith helped him achieve this better mental health, he wants to keep it going. He goes to evensong from time to time and meditates every day – and if he has any inkling of his depression descending, his first line of defence is to get out the map, and plan a mini-pilgrimage.

15

The Widower who made it out of grief's darkest wood

When Joseph Luzzi suffered an unthinkable loss, he found his solace in two people: his mother Yolanda, and an Italian poet who lived 700 years ago.

Joseph Luzzi, professor of Italian literature, was teaching his class at the university when a security guard came to the door. 'My first thought was, I've done nothing wrong,' remembers Joe. He hadn't; but he was about to go through one of the hardest human experiences it is possible to imagine.

That morning, Joe had kissed his pregnant wife Katherine goodbye and headed into work. An hour or so later, she left the house too, on a shopping trip. It should only have taken her a short while, and then she would have returned to their home and to getting things ready for the nursery and the imminent arrival of their first child.

 ## Forty five minutes after Isabel was born, Katherine died

But as Katherine pulled out of a petrol station near her home in upstate New York, her car was in a collision with a van. When paramedics found her, she was huddled over her belly, as though trying to protect her child. She was rushed to hospital, where doctors did all they could to save her. They also carried out an emergency caesarean to deliver the baby girl she was carrying – so soon after Joe was being given the terrible news at the university that his wife had been involved in a horrible road accident, his daughter was – unbeknown to him – born. 'Forty five minutes after Isabel was born, Katherine died,' says Joe. 'I had left the house at eight thirty; by noon, I was a widower and a father.'

When Katherine was buried, a week later, Joe says he felt as though part of himself was going down into the ground with the wife he had loved so much, and who had always been so full of life and fun. But one thing he knew was that he couldn't give up: he had his baby, Isabel, to live for. But living – and living with a small baby, who he had no idea how to look after – was going to be very tough indeed.

Joe grew up in the US, but his family's roots go deep into the countryside of Calabria in southern Italy, the land his parents left soon before his birth, but the place they were always connected with by an invisible umbilical cord. He had been raised, he says, in a Calabrian village that just happened to be in New York state; and in the unbelievably shocking circumstances in which he found himself, that village rallied round. On the day he was able to bring Isabel home from the special care unit, his four sisters and his mother went with him to collect her. And a few months later, when he decided to leave the home he and Katherine had set up, and to raise Isabel instead in Rhode Island, he wasn't alone: with him as he made the drive, sitting in the back seat next to the baby, was his elderly mother Yolanda. As they drove up the highway, Joe recalls, his mother was holding Isabel's tiny hand, singing to her in a Calabrian accent he could barely understand:

'*Chi e sa piccerella, sa piccerella bella.*' she was saying. Who is this little girl, this beautiful little girl? Co-parenting his child with his mother, when he had expected to be co-parenting with his beautiful young wife, was far from easy; but Joe knows how absolutely fundamental his mother's contribution was to getting him and his daughter through the roughest of times. In many ways, he says, Yolanda's

> The family's move to the US had been the biggest shift of her life, but it had prepared her for the unexpected final act of motherhood that Katherine's death would press on her

whole life had been preparing her for this task: she had been raised on a farm in Italy, had fallen in love with and married Joe's father aged 15, and had six children. The family's move to the US had been the biggest shift of her life, but it had prepared her for the unexpected final act of motherhood that Katherine's death would press on her. The day she heard what had happened, says Joe, his mother knew what she had to do.

Yolanda, says her son, is the kind of Catholic whose faith is so connected to her culture and her life that it is impossible to distinguish it from the rest of her existence. Her faith, and her spirituality, is simply part of her: and it was a part she was able to draw on now to help her son and her granddaughter. And the strange thing, Joe admits, is that while he had spent much of his life trying to run away from his family's traditional ways, he now realised how deeply he and his child needed the deep wells of nourishment and love that Yolanda brought, and which were rooted in her background and her faith and her past. 'What had been oppressive to me in my youth and earlier adulthood was now bounty for me and my daughter,' he says. 'I was finally able to embrace the gift that was the centuries of Calabrian maternal wisdom Yolanda Luzzi carried in her five-foot, two-inch, one-hundred-and-ten-pound frame.'

But while Yolanda and centuries of Calabrian mothering were providing a cocoon for Isabel, Joe had to look somewhere else to assuage his grief. As an academic he had long specialised in Italy's central poet Dante, and in the emotional mayhem of the months and years after Katherine's death, he threw himself into his work. He expected

Dante could help him by providing him with a distraction, an absorbing other life in which to bury himself while he tried to heal from the grief of losing his wife; but instead, something remarkable happened. Dante, whose great poem *The Divine Comedy* tells the story of the soul's journey towards God, became not his distraction but his salvation. 'I had turned to books about death and loss but nothing I read really spoke to me,' he says.

'And then I realised that Dante had gone through exactly what I was going through. His muse Beatrice dies, and she becomes his guide in the Divine Comedy. He lost his great love, and I lost my great love. And where Dante truly spoke to me was where he writes about the experience of exile: in the middle of life's journey, he says, he finds himself in a dark wood. He was a guy who had everything: he was a leading poet, a politician, he was living in one of the most exciting cities in the world, and then suddenly he was kicked out and his name was defamed. For the last 20 years of his life he wandered around Italy, banished from his beloved Florence. And that's exactly what the loss of my wife felt like: I felt I was being banished from the life I was expecting to have, cut off from it just at its most wonderful moment.'

For a long time, says Joe, he was where Dante was in his poem: in the dark wood, buried in grief, unable to see the light for all the branches. But eventually, led by Dante, he realised that in order to move on with his life he had to accept that nothing could ever be the same as it had been, either for him or

> I realised I had to let the person I was, or at least a part of him, die along with Katherine, and then I had to build a new life

for his child, now Katherine was dead. 'I realised I had to let the person I was, or at least a part of him, die along with Katherine, and then I had to build a new life,' he says.

It took Joe a long time to get out of his dark wood, but with the help of his daughter and his mother, he did. And then, four years ago, a new woman arrived in his life, an English musician called Helena; taking her to meet Isabel, then three years old, was he says the most momentous introduction he ever made in his life. At last, from within the dark wood he was starting to see a clearing. Dante, he says, had taken his journey to the underworld on Good Friday, implying that his life too would be resurrected by Easter time. As Christ said, if the kernel of wheat died, it would bear much fruit. For a long time, he had watched his life follow Katherine into the ground, wondering whether it would ever bear fruit: now, suddenly, that time had come.

> You can love somebody without a body in a certain way, but that you must reserve your truest love for somebody whose breath you can hear and feel – your child's, your wife's – and that you may visit the underworld but you cannot live there

Today Joe and Helena are married, and as well as ten-year-old Isabel they have James, who's three, and Annabel, 14 months. Dante, says Joe in his memoir, 'taught me that you can love somebody without a body in a certain way, but that you must reserve your truest love for somebody whose breath you can hear and feel – your child's, your wife's – and that you may visit the underworld but you cannot live there.' He has left the trees behind him, although he knows how easily any of us can be pulled into their darkness; and every day, he says, he is truly thankful for all that he has, and for making it through.

Joe, Helena and Isabel

16

The Anglican priest whose own terrible injuries led him to work with people with trauma across the world

Fr Michael Lapsley was an anti-apartheid campaigner who was targeted by pro-apartheid activists, and lost both his hands in a letter bomb. But his own experience became the root of his work for others.

The bomber who targeted Fr Michael Lapsley thought carefully about how to kill him: the device was concealed in a religious magazine, and triggered to explode when the priest opened it. It was a postal bomb, and it arrived while Fr Lapsley was travelling. He collected a pile of letters and packages from the post office on his return, and went through them gradually over the next few days. The moment when the bomb exploded has never left him: 'It was pain on a scale that I didn't think a human being could ever experience,' he says. 'I was thrown back by the force of it; and I knew straightaway that my hands were gone.'

There was such loss: the loss of my hands, which will never return, the loss of my eye. This is a permanent dimension to my life; it affects every part of my life

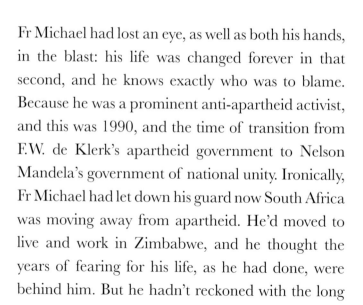

Fr Michael had lost an eye, as well as both his hands, in the blast: his life was changed forever in that second, and he knows exactly who was to blame. Because he was a prominent anti-apartheid activist, and this was 1990, and the time of transition from F.W. de Klerk's apartheid government to Nelson Mandela's government of national unity. Ironically, Fr Michael had let down his guard now South Africa was moving away from apartheid. He'd moved to live and work in Zimbabwe, and he thought the years of fearing for his life, as he had done, were behind him. But he hadn't reckoned with the long shadow of apartheid, and he hadn't reckoned with a letter bomb.

Today, 28 years on, Fr Michael is adept with his prosthetic limbs. He's sparky and cheerful, and seems much younger than 69: so how much does that experience, of being the victim of a bomber, define him now? 'Grief,' he says, 'is always there, somewhere. There was such loss: the loss of my hands, which will never return, the loss of my eye. This is a permanent dimension to my life; it affects every part of my life.' And yet, he says, it has deepened his faith: 'I had a sense of God being present with me in that experience.' What's even more remarkable, though, is that he says the bomb was in some ways 'redemptive...because life is like a river.

When something terrible happens, our life becomes like a whirlpool. And you become like a prisoner at that time, you're caught in the whirlpool.' Now, though, the whirlpool has subsided; Fr Michael has learnt to swim again in the river, and he's swimming in a river in which he's able to use his experiences to help others who, like him, have experienced great trauma: he established an organisation called the

Institute for Healing of Memories, and he tours the world running workshops for people who have been caught up in terrible events, and who need to come to terms with the resulting agonies and feelings.

Fr Michael was born, not in the South Africa whose story would become so entwined with his own, but 7000 miles away in New Zealand. He was raised there in a church-going family, and as a young man he felt called to the religious life. He went to Australia to join an Anglican religious order, and was ordained there in 1973. Later that year, his order transferred him to Durban in South Africa to study: and it was there that his life was to change forever.

The shock was apartheid, the rawness of it and the reality of it. Fr Michael tells the story of how, newly arrived, he decided to go to the post office to send his mother a telegram to reassure her that he'd arrived safely. When he got there, he realised there were two entrances: one for 'whites' and the other for 'non-whites'. 'The colour of my skin was defining everything,' he remembers. 'I felt it was like leprosy: if I could wash it off, I could become a human being again.'

What he quickly realised, in his new life in South Africa, was that all whites benefitted from apartheid, that all blacks were damaged by it – but that everyone, regardless of their colour, was a prisoner of it. He knew he had to devote his life to working to overturn it, especially because, to his horror, he

> That was what really shocked me - the realisation that apartheid went under the name of Christianity

realised that it was underpinned by a belief that it was Christian. 'That was what really shocked me - the realisation that apartheid went under the name of Christianity. They claimed divine guidance for what came to be called a crime against humanity and what we in the faith community call heresy. So apartheid was not simply justice, human rights or social justice: it was a faith issue, too.'

He became chaplain to three different universities: one of them for white students, the others for non-whites – that gave him, he says, a helpful perspective across the issues of the communities. When students began to protest and were killed by the apartheid regime, Fr Michael began to speak out against the system: he was expelled, went to live in Lesotho, and joined the African National Congress. And then, in the early 1980s, he moved to Harare: and it was there, in 1990, that the letter bomb arrived.

> Coming to terms with his own wounds, and learning to move ahead with life despite them, gave him the strength to do the same on a wider scale, for the people around him

He was hospitalised for months, first in Zimbabwe and then in Australia; and it was clear he would not be able to return to his work as a parish priest. And so, in 1992, he returned to South Africa, where he could not help but be struck by the fact that just as he was injured, and had been traumatised, by what had happened to him, so the whole of that country had been injured, and remained traumatised, by the history of apartheid. 'There are so many signs, still, that South Africa is suffering,' he says. 'The events of several hundred years still affects lives there today. You see it in the scale of domestic, family and sexual violence, for example.'

Coming to terms with his own wounds, and learning to move ahead with life despite them, gave him the strength to do the same on a wider scale, for the people around him. 'The way we respond to our own wounds can enable us to walk beside others provided we are addressing our own woundedness,' he says. 'When I came back to South Africa the first thing that struck me was that we were a damaged nation. And we all had a story to tell.'

Today Fr Michael's life is about listening to those stories, illuminating others' experiences with his own perspective, and helping people find the safe places they need to be able to explore the grief and trauma of their lives. The Institute for Healing of Memories works extensively in South Africa, but he has taken his approach and expertise to other communities that have known mass trauma too: Rwanda in the aftermath of the genocide, New York after 9/11. He has seen time and again, he says, how much good can come out of these terrible events. 'Redeeming the past is about how we bring life out of death, good out of evil,' he says.

He's put the same philosophy very much into force in his own life, too. He firmly believes that the person who sent the letter bomb lost more than he did in the blast. 'Part of what I do now is to live in as joyful and as full a way as I can,' he explains.

 When I think about what happened, I keep this in my mind: I lost a lot, I still have a lot, and I gained a lot because of it

'Because there's something so cold-blooded about sending a letter bomb. The person who sent that sat down and thought, how can I kill this priest? And the thing is that he failed – he failed to kill me. So I live my life to the full. When I think about what happened, I keep this in my mind: I lost a lot, I still have a lot, and I gained a lot because of it.'

17

The Mother saved from depression by words

Rachel Kelly was looking after her two young children when mental illness hit; and in the months and years that followed, she discovered a lifeline in the Bible and poetry.

Rachel Kelly was in an acute state of depression – suicidal and in a psychiatric hospital – when she first got an inkling that words could save her. 'I'd had a lot of drugs and I was in a terribly anxious state, screaming that I wanted to die and clinging onto my husband, who was on one side of me, and my mother, who was on the other. I'd totally given up hope: I didn't think the drugs would work, and I didn't think I wanted to carry on. And suddenly my mother started murmuring: "My grace is sufficient for thee, for my power is perfected in weakness".

And those words felt like the first stirring of hope: up to that point it had all seemed impossible, but this seemed like a shard of something positive, something I could cling on to. I began to repeat it; instead of screaming that I wanted to die, I said what she'd said.'

> Rachel describes how, in times of need, two lines from *Invictus* by WE Henley can make all the difference to what happens next: 'I am the master of my fate/I am the captain of my soul'

The words that became the beacons of Rachel's harbour are from St Paul's Letter to the Corinthians, in the New Testament. And when her mother realised the power of repeating words, mantra-like, she sought out more. 'She would drip-feed me little lines of poetry – it was like chicken soup for the soul,' remembers Rachel. 'One of her favourite poets was the 18th century Welsh-born priest and devotional poet George Herbert, and there are some incredible lines: "Grief melts away/like snow in May/as if there were no such cold thing...", from a poem called *The Flower*. I kept repeating those lines, and they spelled out hope to me: they're about renewal and rebirth, and I started to know that, as Herbert goes on to say, my shrivelled heart would recover its greenness.' What was so powerful, says Kelly, was that Herbert described desolation – but also recovery. 'He held my hands across the century and said to me, you are going to be ok,' she says.

Today Rachel is ok: and she's keen to share the power of poetry as a tool for better mental health. Even now she's recovered and calm, she has her wobbles – as we all do – and reciting lines of poetry is grounding, validating, and connects us to other human beings who have felt what we are feeling in this moment. Poetry we've learned to recite means we have another voice – inside us but not of us – that's always there, ready to be pulled out of the box wherever we are and whenever it's required, a kind of on-board first responder in times of psychological need. There's also a certainty and stability about being able to conjure up those words: they're a crutch, we can lean on them, they can even do the thinking for us. Rachel describes how, in times of need, two lines from *Invictus* by WE Henley can make all the difference to what happens next: 'I am the master of my fate/I am the captain of my soul'. And when things were really bad, and all she could hear in her head were negative voices, she could effectively drown them out by repeating, over and over, positive lines from poetry and scripture: they became substitutions, life-giving mantras rather than life-sapping ones.

The irony was that, in the moment when she was hit by mental ill health, Rachel Kelly looked like one of the luckiest women alive. She'd grown up in west London, been educated at St Paul's Girls' School and at Oxford University, and married Sebastian, a banker. She was working as a journalist at *The Times*, and the mother of two small boys, when she hit her first serious spell of depression. In her bestselling book *Black Rainbow: How Words Healed Me*, she describes how she had just bathed her boys – Edward was then two, and George was three months – and was blowing raspberries on their tummies and laughing with them.

But when they went to bed, the cloud descended. Rachel felt her pulse racing, and had a weird, disembodied sensation. She was hearing words she didn't realise she was speaking; and suddenly, she felt she was in a plummeting plane that was about to crash.

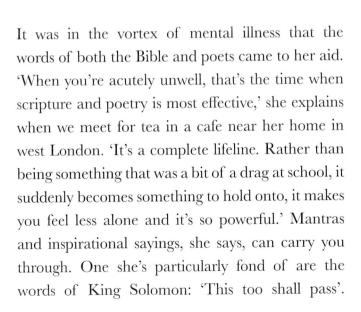

It's a complete lifeline. Rather than being something that was a bit of a drag at school, it suddenly becomes something to hold onto, it makes you feel less alone and it's so powerful

It was in the vortex of mental illness that the words of both the Bible and poets came to her aid. 'When you're acutely unwell, that's the time when scripture and poetry is most effective,' she explains when we meet for tea in a cafe near her home in west London. 'It's a complete lifeline. Rather than being something that was a bit of a drag at school, it suddenly becomes something to hold onto, it makes you feel less alone and it's so powerful.' Mantras and inspirational sayings, she says, can carry you through. One she's particularly fond of are the words of King Solomon: 'This too shall pass'.

Because, she says, they remind you that it's not only the sad times that pass; the happy times pass as well.

The mood in the room can suddenly change when an inmate makes an emotional connection with the work in hand

So poetry came to her aid, and a few good years followed; years that brought three more children, another daughter and then twins. But what Rachel hadn't realised, she says now, is that if you've suffered serious depression at one point in your life, you're at greater risk of it coming back – and if it does return, it's likely to be worse the second time around. In 2003, six years after her initial episode, depression came back with a vengeance – and this time, it took two years to get through the fog. And, she explains, you don't recover in a flash; it's more like a Himalayan climb, and there are periods when you go down as well as up.

As she recovered, Rachel put her reporting skills to work researching mental illness; and decided to make working to overcome it, and the stigma surrounding it, a central part of her life. Today, in addition to writing about depression and how to deal with it, she runs workshops for vulnerable groups – including poetry writing workshops for prisoners. These can, she says, bring unexpected moments of magical inspiration for all those taking part. 'The mood in the room can suddenly change when an inmate makes an emotional connection with the work in hand,' she explains. 'I always leave the prison with some new insight or having discovered a new writer. Some of the prisoners – often the older men – have heads richly stocked with poetry which they have shared in the group enriching us all.'

Her passion, she says, is sharing the ways we can all look after our mental health – and know the danger signs to look out for. 'That's why I run workshops and write about it – because if you know how to look after yourself, you can prevent some of the problems. If I'd known then what I know now, I could perhaps have prevented the second breakdown I suffered.' A combination of stigma and a lack of NHS resources, she believes, contribute to our current high levels of mental ill health – but her work is all about empowerment, and spreading the word about what we can each do as individuals in our own lives to look after ourselves.

Through it all, her faith has helped sustain her. 'It's a bit like the war,' she says. 'There are no atheists in the trenches. When the chips are down,

> Rather than feeling ashamed, I felt the sense that only God is perfect - so it's fine to admit our shortcomings as human beings

you turn to God. My faith was so important, I clung onto it for dear life. And so many of the tenets of the Catholicism in which I'd been raised resonated: forgiveness, forgiving ourselves as well as others. Rather than feeling ashamed, I felt the sense that only God is perfect – so it's fine to admit our shortcomings as human beings.'

Above it all, though, it was the poetry of the Bible and particularly of religious and spiritual poetry that carried her through. 'The language and beauty of the words of the Church and of the Bible is so beautiful,' she says. 'Whenever I'm in trouble, I turn to it – there's this timelessness, this sense of connection. It really helps.'

18

The nun who's a friend to sex workers

Ancy Mathew's order was set up to help women working in prostitution – today, its members are also on the frontline of the battle against human trafficking.

It's a bright afternoon, but the blinds of the basement flat are tightly shut. The young women who live here inhabit a twilight world rarely penetrated by the rays of the sun or the eyes of others: their reality is right here beside a busy street in west London, but their existence goes unnoticed.

In part that's because it's how they want it to be: that's why they keep their curtains drawn. But in another sense it suits the world, as well as the girls, that they are hidden.

Sister Ancy Mathew knocks at the door: it's opened swiftly and we slip quickly inside, our eyes adjusting to the semi-darkness of a neat, anonymous sitting room with its white leather sofas, giant TV screen and coffee-coloured rug. Lucy, who has let us in, is in her mid-twenties, and is wearing a fluffy dressing gown over patterned leggings. Lucy isn't her real name, but it's the only name anyone in Britain knows

My husband, my mother, my children – none of them know what I am doing here

her by. Her true identity, like the fact that she plies the world's oldest profession, is her best-kept secret. Back home in eastern Europe, where she's from, no-one knows what Lucy's life in London is about. 'My husband, my mother, my children – none of them know what I am doing here,' she says. 'I've told them I've got a good job in the tourist industry, and I send a large part of the money I earn home to them. It means my daughters will have an education and a future – they won't have to do what I'm doing, it's their ticket to a better life than the one I've had.'

Lucy's life, and the lives of her two flatmates, are of

necessity disconnected from the world around them. Their English is not good; they have no other friends in London. Because they don't have 'normal' jobs in shops or offices, there is no new network for them to become part of now they have moved here. So they are lonely, and isolated; the only visitors to this flat are those who come here to pay for sex. Sister Ancy is one of the very few, and perhaps even the only, outsider who has access to Lucy's world. Inside the flat, the pair greet one another with a hug and a kiss.

This is working on the frontline for an Adoratrice sister in 2014. The order was founded in Madrid in 1856 by St Maria Micaela, with the twin aims of worshipping Christ, and freeing women working in prostitution or other situations that enslave them. Today there are more than 1,100 Adoratrices working in 23 countries throughout the world. The Spanish-speaking countries are their heartland; but they have had a small but significant presence in the UK since the 1950s, and today a handful of their sisters live in central London. Among them is Sister Ancy; and over the last few years, very quietly and without any fanfare, she has been pioneering a new project alongside the Metropolitan Police that has helped transform the work of its trafficking unit.

Sister Ancy was born in Kerala in India in the 1960s. After joining the order she worked for some years in Calcutta with street children, many of whom had been born to sex worker mothers. Her move to London in 2000 was a wrench, but she accepted the challenge. But her new surroundings, in one of the most privileged corners of the city, made her wonder how she could possibly put her order's charism into action. 'I thought, what is God's plan in living out the mission of our founder here?' she says. 'I knew there would be a way.'

There was. Within a few months of arriving at the Adoratrice convent, Sister Ancy and another sister in her community had become part of a team of religious sisters from different congregations who work with women of the street in Kings Cross in central London. 'We worked alongside the women, trying to provide support and healthcare and a welcome for them,' she says. 'It was good work and valuable work, but I felt it wasn't quite enough of a challenge.'

After prayer and reflection, she felt there had to be 'something more' that could be done – especially for the most vulnerable women who were being sexually exploited, those who had been trafficked into the UK and who were effectively sex slaves. Like all those who work in her field, she was increasingly aware of the growth of trafficking – according to the National Crime Agency (NCA) its incidence has risen sharply in recent years. By its very nature its true extent is hidden, and it's likely that the figure

 I thought, what is God's plan in living out the mission of our founder here?

of 5,000 reported by the NCA in 2018 is merely the tip of the iceberg. Most of those trafficked are from Romania, Poland and Albania, with others being brought into the country from Africa or Asia. In many cases they travel to the UK with men they believe are their boyfriends, only to be coerced into prostitution once they arrive.

In 2010 the Metropolitan Police set up its human trafficking unit, and its founding head was Catholic Kevin Hyland, a senior police officer who had previously worked in homicide, gun crime and organised robbery: many people have been rescued from slavery as a result, but they are often in a state of extreme trauma, and need very careful and specialist care.

That was the issue that led Sister Ancy to set up a charity called Rahab (named after a Hebrew woman in the Bible who was a sex worker). She teamed up with the officers from the Human Trafficking unit, going with them on raids to flats where trafficked women might be being held, and providing support and accommodation to any women who were found in their most vulnerable early days.

It's hard going, and the tiny Sister Ancy cuts a diminutive figure alongside the burly police officers with whom she works. Her calling, she says, is to be there for the women: when a raid is ongoing she will wait outside in the police vehicle until the situation has been assessed by the police, and then go into the house or flat to talk to the women inside. 'Sometimes they have been trafficked, but often they have not,' she says. 'But either way we offer friendship, support; someone who is there just for them, to listen with compassion and understanding.'

From the police point of view, the presence of the

Rahab team at police raids is nothing short of a gift from God. 'What's especially difficult in this work is that we're police officers, and the women who've been trafficked have often been taught that they can't trust the police or the authorities – that's one of the ways in which their captors keep them in check,' explains Detective Sergeant Phil Rashidi

> The first 24 to 48 hours after we find someone who's been trafficked are crucial for us in our investigation, and they're also extremely difficult for the women

of the human trafficking unit. 'All people who've been trafficked are extremely vulnerable, and you inevitably find they've been let down throughout their lives and trusting anyone is really hard. So for us, having Sister Ancy and her team means we can hand them on to people who they really can trust – religious sisters.' Many of the women have been part of a church community at home, and whereas a police officer might be a threat, a nun would not be. 'The first 24 to 48 hours after we find someone who's been trafficked are crucial for us in our investigation, and they're also extremely difficult for the women,' says Rashidi. 'They have to move out of the place where they've been living, sometimes for some time, and they are probably going to be cut off from the people they've had around them. We know how traumatic all that will be, but we can't provide

It's hard to overestimate how important the work of Sister Ancy and Rahab is

care for them round the clock – if we didn't have Rahab and its safe houses to provide emergency accommodation, we'd have to put them into hotels. But they'd be alone there, and that's the last thing they need at that particular time.'

Being in the care of people they know they can trust means the women are far more likely to open up about the information that can prove crucial to the police in making arrests and in steering successful prosecutions. 'It's hard to overestimate how important the work of Sister Ancy and Rahab is,' says Rashidi. 'In the past we used to operate in a kind of silo fashion, but then we realised that this is holistic work; it's about whole people.' And what the police were finding hard to provide – the human support and friendship – Rahab has been able to give.

You get the sense, talking to Rashidi and his colleagues, that the Rahab presence has transformed their work. What it means, too, is that where women are found to be working but not illegally, they don't get left without support. 'If the police go into a flat and the women there aren't trafficked, we can still follow them in and talk to the women and offer friendship,' says Sister Ancy.

Which brings us back to Lucy and her flatmates, and to the many other flats visited on a regular basis by Sister Ancy and her co-workers at Rahab. 'West London is full of working flats, often quite invisible to the world around them,' she explains. 'Our mission is about supporting the women. My life is about prayer, and about being with the women: they are no worse than me and no better than me, they are my equals and that is how I treat them.'

And it's abundantly clear, accompanying Sister

Ancy on her rounds, how important her role is. In one flat we meet Blessing from Ghana: she has been in Britain for many years, she runs a flat occupied by four or five sex workers, and like Georgina her family have no idea about her real occupation. But she has had enough: she is keen to get out. 'You're the one person who knows all about me,' Blessing tells Sister Ancy. 'It's going to be very difficult giving up this job because I earn a lot of money through it, far more than I do in my other job.' Sister Ancy knows how hard that will be, but she absolutely believes Blessing can move forward with the right support – and she promises to be there for her, whatever happens in the months and years ahead.

It's that total support, from someone who is completely dedicated to the task, that makes Sister Ancy's contribution so invaluable. 'The fact is that we're all paid to do this – it's our job,' says one of the police officers. 'But for trafficked women and other sex workers, it's their whole lives and their whole situation – and having someone like Sister Ancy, who is dedicating her whole life to it and who isn't doing it because it's her job, means the world to all of us and to all of them.'

19

The activist nun who's changing hearts and minds

Sister Teresa Forcades saw a lack of humanity in the world around her – and instead of remaining silent, she chose to speak out.

Teresa Forcades is a Benedictine nun, and she has a confession to make. 'Sometimes,' she says, 'when I am in church, reading from the lectern, I have to leave out a sentence from the text because I find it too offensive.' The example she gives is from Paul's first letter to Timothy (2:12): 'I permit no woman to teach or have authority over a man: she is to keep silent.'

Sister Teresa is certainly not keeping silent. The future of Europe, feminism, democracy, nationalism, the failings of the Church: on all these issues and many more, Forcades has a view and is not averse to sharing it. She's been described as one of the most radical thinkers of the moment; she's a frequent commentator on Spanish TV, and has long been a leading figure in the campaign for Catalonian independence.

It's four years since Forcades co-authored, with economist Arcadi Oliveres, a blueprint for Catalonian independence. Explaining her reasons in *The Guardian* at the time, she wrote: 'A smaller political unit allows for a more humane political experience. In a smaller country, social activists and people working at the grassroots level have a greater chance of knowing each other personally and being able to pass on to each other relevant information in a direct manner; they also have a greater chance of knowing most of their political representatives personally.'

She expands on this point when we meet. She has no doubt, she explains, that nationalism, and what it means for Europe, is one of the central issues of our age. 'We have to pay attention to our roots, but not in a xenophobic way.' Democracy has 'become confused so it means representational democracy only: we need to get the power back into our hands. I say back, but I'm not sure we ever had it. Political units that are smaller make more sense to me. They might be able to incorporate democracy in a more direct way.'

Thank you, God, for making me an atheist

Being direct, in touch and connected seem hallmark Forcades traits: in person she's open, straightforward and fun. Raised in Barcelona, she was the eldest of three daughters born to a poet and a nurse. She was baptised into the Church but it was a formality only: her parents were not believers, and had little time for Catholicism. 'It was 1966 and Franco had already arranged for the monarchy to take over after he died. When I was growing up, my parents told me the Church was like the monarchy – an institution of the past.' But when she was 15 she read the Gospels for the first time. 'And after I'd finished I felt a sense of indignation. I felt I'd wasted 15 years of my life because I didn't know there was a God.' Her teenage rebellion, she laughs, was 'to believe';

one of her father's frequent sayings has been the curious 'Thank you, God, for making me an atheist.' And Forcades thinks she's finally, in her early fifties, beginning to understand what he means. 'I think he's saying that there's a possibility of being open to a transcendence, without putting a name to it. Because putting a name to God often does Her a disservice.'

Who does the taking care of people in our communities? Is it a private matter, or is it a matter for all of us?

When she was 11 her parents divorced, and because it was a cheaper and more practical option, she was sent to a convent school. Until this point she'd been educated in a Catalan-speaking school; now, she was taught in Spanish. Thrilled by her new-found enthusiasm for God, the nuns thought she was a shoo-in for the novitiate; Forcades had other ideas. 'I thought, no way. I'd read about Vatican II and I thought, this is the time for laypeople in the Church.' At the age of ten, in her Catalan school, she'd told a teacher one day that she wanted to follow her mother into nursing; the teacher challenged her, said 'Why not be a doctor?', and a seed was sown. After school she went to medical school in Barcelona, before moving to New York to work as a hospital doctor in the early 1990s. What she experienced there shocked her: the first question patients were asked was 'Are your insurance payments up to date?' It wasn't the question Forcades wanted to ask; today, she says the 'ethics of care' – who is responsible for health and other care in society – is one of the burning questions of our times. 'Who does the taking care of people in our communities? Is it a private matter, or is it a matter for all of us?' It's pretty clear where she stands on the subject.

In the mid 1990s she returned to Spain to study for her final medical exams; she needed somewhere quiet to work, and someone suggested the Benedictine convent in Montserrat. Forcades surprised herself during her stay by feeling strangely drawn to the nuns' life; when the abbess asked her one day to talk to the sisters about her work with patients with Aids, she decided to set them a test. 'I talked about aspects of the gay community, and I thought will the nuns just ignore that part of my talk? At the end the hands went up: the first to speak was a 92-year-old nun, and her question was all about gay people and how they were treated. The sisters didn't see issues, they saw people.' Forcades knew this was the life for her; but first, she returned to the US where she was now studying at Harvard, before entering the monastery in Montserrat in 1997. At first, she says, she was put in the workshop making the ceramics the nuns sell to make their living. 'But I wasn't very good at ceramics, and even when they put me in charge of looking after the sick sisters, I wasn't very good at that either.' What she was good at, it turned out, was giving lectures and talks and becoming politically active in the Catalan independence movement, and after a while she moved to do this full-time.

Being a nun, though, remains fundamental to everything else; she comes from that tradition of independently-minded, polymath, intellectual, radicals that include historical figures like Hildegard of Bingen, Hilda of Whitby and Juana Ines de la Cruz, and contemporary characters like Simone Campbell and Helen Prejean. As for them, feminism is a given: like many other Catholic feminists, she prefers to wait for the truth to be revealed, rather than obsessing about her cause. 'Of course I would like a Church that is not sexist,' she says. 'There is a sin in the Church called structural misogyny: they say, you can only be in decision-making positions if you are ordained, and you can only be ordained if you are a man. That does not reflect the Gospels.' But life in a monastery has brought illumination. 'In our monastery, women are in charge. In our daily life there are no men, and the abbess is *in persona Christi*.'

Of course I would like a Church that is not sexist

Although many would argue that Francis has been slow to tackle structural misogyny in the Catholic Church, Forcades is quietly hopeful. 'He's set up the commission for deacons – and even though some feel that's just a strategy to throw us a few crumbs, I still think it will bring opportunities.' But her main reason for optimism under Francis is this: under the pontificates of Benedict XVI and John Paul II, she says, her abbess was often on the receiving end of letters of complaint from the Vatican about her unruly nun. Since 2013 the letters have dried up completely; and as far as Forcades is concerned, that silence is deafening.

20

The Kennedy who runs the Special Olympics

Tim Shriver's aunt, who had learning disabilities, is his beacon.

Tim Shriver is every inch a Kennedy – tall, handsome, commanding – and he knows all about the family traits that have made his family the Royalty of US politics (his uncle JFK was president; another uncle, Bobby, also assassinated, was attorney general). But what's less well known is why his family has had such a cherished connection with people with learning disabilities, for whom his mother Eunice Shriver, President Kennedy's sister, founded the Special Olympics in 1968. They involve thousands of athletes from all over the world – and what every competitor has in common is that they suffer from a learning disability.

So why have so many Kennedys, including him, devoted so much of their time to working for people who are intellectually disadvantaged? It all comes down, he explains, to another of President Kennedy's sisters: his aunt Rosemary. For many years, Rosemary was the 'secret' Kennedy: the third of the nine children of Joseph P Kennedy, who was American ambassador to London in the

> **It was a time when most people with learning difficulties would have been institutionalised from childhood**

1930s, and his wife Rose, she had an intellectual disability and was hardly ever seen in public with the rest of the clan. She grew up, says Shriver, at a time when there was enormous shame surrounding people with special needs – people didn't want to admit to it.

For the Kennedys, with their endless quest for success and their boundless ambition, Rosemary's existence was a special difficulty: and when she was 23, and because her condition seemed to be getting worse, her father Joseph made a terrible decision. Without consulting Rose or any of the rest of the family, he booked Rosemary in for a lobotomy: but the brain operation went horribly wrong, and Rosemary was left with only limited motor and speaking skills.

The staunchly Catholic Kennedys had Rosemary cared for by the nuns in an institution in Wisconsin, where she died in 2005. But for many years, says Tim Shriver, who is 59, his aunt was a regular visitor to their home – and she taught him, and the wider family, an invaluable lesson in what matters most in life. 'We were a very competitive family with a lot of ambitious people and quite an aggressive attitude – there was always a big determination to perform, and to succeed,' he remembers.

Rosemary, though, wasn't able to compete the way the rest of the family did: and though her father Joseph made the decision to have her lobotomised, he and the rest of the Kennedys had earlier fought to keep her at home. 'It was a time when most people with learning difficulties would have been institutionalised from childhood, but my aunt grew up with her brothers and sisters,' says Shriver.

And what that gave them, he says, was a sense of conscience, and an understanding that not everyone in the world was as fortunate, or as strong, as they were – and also, that people who were weaker need help, and that it was their duty to provide that help. 'I honestly think that this experience, of having Rosemary as their sister, was what gave President Kennedy and Robert Kennedy their strong sense of justice and guided their determination to help those who needed help in the world,' he says. 'My Uncle Ted confirmed that to me, and said that Rosemary provided the spiritual grounding to his own development and determination to do good through politics.

'Rosemary was the spiritual blueprint of the Kennedys: she was at the heart of their understanding about why they had to work for those who weren't powerful in the world.' In some ways, he says, she was the most important Kennedy of them all – because it was through her example that the most powerful members of the family got their determination to help others. 'Their legacy was always about those who society excluded, and that all comes back to Rosemary,' he says.

Shriver says his own experience of working with the Special Olympics also brought him an epiphany of understanding what life is really all about. 'My mother had founded the Special Olympics, and it was obvious to me that it was a good thing, and I could see I had a moral responsibility to it and that getting involved with it was something I was expected to do,' he says.

> Quite simply, it made me realise the true value of individuals: the true value of myself, and the true value of others

'But what I found turned my life around, because what I encountered through the athletes of the Special Olympics was a whole new way of seeing life and a whole way of s eing myself in the world. Quite simply, it made me realise the true value of individuals: the true value of myself, and the true value of others.

'Like most people, somewhere inside I believed that what made me matter were the big things in life, the things my family had always told me were important: the influence and the wealth and the string of academic degrees, all of that. I thought, like most people do, that to be someone of value I had to be someone with something interesting to say, or something witty to say, or someone who was

> They made me stop in my tracks to really think about what it is to be a human being, and they made me fall in love with life – and then I fell in love with God, the life and the presence of all things

clever. But meeting the Special Olympics athletes taught me that it's not about any of those things, it's simply about accepting others and being with them, walking alongside them.

'They made me stop in my tracks to really think about what it is to be a human being, and they made me fall in love with life – and then I fell in love with God, the life and the presence of all things. He told me, you can't just love people with money or political influence or celebrity credentials, you have to love everyone in the world.'

Further Information

Jessica Cox
Jessica's website is at *www.jessicacox.com*

Margaret Mizen
The Mizen family's website to create a living legacy of forgiveness, peace and hope for their son is at *www.forjimmy.org*

Pierluigi Molla
For more information on the life and legacy of St Gianna Beretta Molla see *www.saintgianna.org*

Magnus MacFarlane-Barrow
For more information on Mary's Meals, go to *www.marysmeals.org*

Helen Prejean
www.sisterhelen.org

Sunny Jacobs and Peter Pringle
For more information about the story of Sunny and Peter, and the work they now do, see *www.sunnyandpeter.com*

Terri Roberts
Terri's book *Forgiven: The Amish School Shooting, a Mother's Love, and a Story of Remarkable Grace*, is published by Baker Publishing

Jean Vanier
For more information on Jean's work see *www.jean-vanier.org/en*

Further Information

Fr Angel Garcia
www.mensajerossananton.com

Sister Rita Lee
For more information on the Lalley Centre see *www. caritassalford.org.uk*

Rose Hudson-Wilkin
To learn more about Rose's story, listen to her *Desert Island Discs* at *bbc.co.uk*

Anne-Marie Cockburn
www.anyoneschild.org
Anne-Marie's book *5,742 Days: A Mother's Journey Through Loss* Is published by Infinite Ideas

Christina Noble
The Christina Noble Children's Foundation is at *www.cncf.org*

Guy Stagg
The Crossway by Guy Stagg is published by Pan Macmillan

Joseph Luzzi
In a Dark Wood by Joseph Luzzi is published by William Collins

Fr Michael Lapsley
Learn more about Fr Michael's work and order his book *My Journey from Freedom Fighter to Healer* at *www.healing-memories.org*

Further Information

Rachel Kelly
Learn more about Rachel's work and order her books at
www.rachel-kelly.net

Ancy Mathew
To find out more about the work of Rahab, and to make a
contribution to its work, go to *www.rahabuk.com*
For more on the Adoratrices, see *www.adoratrices.com*

Sister Teresa Forcades
Faith and Freedom by Sister Teresa Forcades is published by
politybooks.com

Tim Shriver
For more information about Timothy Shriver, the Special
Olympics and his book *Fully Alive: Discovering What Matters
Most*, see *www.timothyshriver.com*

**For more books by Alive Publishing visit:
www.alivepublishing.co.uk**

Image Credits

p20 © Kathy Hutchins/shutterstock.com
p30 © Image courtesy of Margaret Mizen
p38 © Magnus PR, courtesy of Kim Webster
p47 © Magnus PR, courtesy of Kim Webster
p48 © NurPhoto/Contributor/Getty Images
p58 © www.petersfraserdunlop.com
p68 © Image courtey of Zachary Roberts
p81 © Image courtesy of Terri Roberts
p82 © Kotukaran/www.commons.wikimedia.org
p91 © Christopher Bremrose/Flickr via sojo.net/articles/
     jean-vanier-prophet-21st-century
p92 © Image courtesy of Pierluigi Molla
p99 © www.saintgianna.org
p100 © Image courtesy of Joanna Moorhead
p110 © Danny Claffey
p119 © www.irishpost.com
p120 © Keith Larby/Alamy Stock Photo
p129 © Peter Marshall/Alamy Stock Photo
p130 © Image courtesy of Anne-Marie Cockburn
p141 © Image courtesy of Anne-Marie Cockburn
p142 © El Keegan/www.irishcountrymagazine.ie
p151 © El Keegan/www.irishcountrymagazine.ie
p152 © Barney Poole
p161 © Image courtesy of Guy Stagg
p162 © Helena Baillie
p171 © Ian Turner
p172 © Rick Eglinton/Contributor/Getty Images
p181 © Richard Lautens/Contributor/Getty Images

Image Credits

p182 © Libi Pedder
p192 © tugolukof/shutterstock.com
p203 © ChameleonsEye/shutterstock.com
p204 © Lídia Pujol/www.flickr.com/photos/lidiapujol
(changed to black and white image)
p212 © ITAR-TASS News Agency/Alamy Stock Photo